FREE TO SPEAK

My Journey from Stuttering to Public Speaking

LARRY STEIN

Free to Speak: My Journey from Stuttering to Public Speaking
Published by Chicago House Publishing, LLC
Deerfield, IL

Copyright ©2024 by Larry Stein. All rights reserved.

Website: SteinOnStuttering.com

No part of this book may be reproduced in any form or by any mechanical means, including information storage and retrieval systems without permission in writing from the publisher/author, except by a reviewer who may quote passages in a review.

All images, logos, quotes, and trademarks included in this book are subject to use according to trademark and copyright laws of the United States of America.

ISBN: 979-8-218-13425-9
SELF-HELP / Personal Growth / General

Cover and interior design by Victoria Wolf, wolfdesignandmarketing.com, copyright owned by Larry Stein.

QUANTITY PURCHASES: Schools, companies, professional groups, clubs, and other organizations may qualify for special terms when ordering quantities of this title. For information, email Larry@SteinOnStuttering.com.

All rights reserved by Larry Stein and Chicago House Publishing, LLC.
Printed in the United States of America.

Quotes from Leaders in the Stuttering and Mental Health Community

"Larry Stein takes you through his personal journey in overcoming the challenges of stuttering and in doing so provides important strategies to help others in their journey. This book is a must-read for anyone who seeks inspiration and scientifically grounded information on how to work through their stuttering."

—Neil H. Pliskin, PhD, Professor Clinical Psychiatry and Neurology, University of Illinois at Chicago

"There are many paths out of the forest of shame, guilt, and struggle that surround many of us who live with stuttering. Larry Stein has shared his own journey in an honest and compelling manner that gives hope to those who have yet to find their own path."

—Dr. Lee Reeves, Retired Veterinarian, Former Chairman of the National Stuttering Association (NSA)

"Larry Stein truly gets it. His suggestions and well-laid plan resonate deeply with me, as his journey closely mirrors my own. If a Top 10 book list existed for people who stutter, I would certainly include this one, it's really special."

—Tom Scharstein, Chair, World Stuttering Network (WSN)

"Free To Speak is about a man's stuttering journey, his struggles, revelations and eventual triumph. It's about finding your strength and your voice. And on top of it all, it also provides you with tools to find your own voice. A must-read, not only for people who stutter, but also for everyone who surrounds them."

—Anita S. Blom, Former Vice Chair of the European League of Stuttering Associations (ELSA)

"Larry invites us all into a world of stuttering from his personal perspective, with the added bonus of invaluable advice and help for those who still seek answers and solutions. A must-read for stutterers, therapists, family, and friends."

—Michael O Shea, Co-Founder of Stuttering Awareness Mental Wellbeing Ireland

"Larry Stein's quest to deal with and ultimately manage his stuttering is an excellent resource for others exploring their own path to improving their speech. I have introduced Larry to a couple of my clients; he offers an intriguing, first-hand perspective on his experience with stuttering."

—Alida Engel, CCC-SLP, BCS-F, Center for Speech and Learning

Quotes from People Who Stutter

"Finally, a raw and authentic book to help people overcome stuttering. After years of speech therapy, meditation and other therapies, it wasn't until I met Larry and worked hard to learn his strategies that I experienced the true freedom of speaking."
—Sarah Nikirk, University Administrator (USA)

"My speech has improved tremendously over the past year working with Larry. For someone who has stuttered for over 35 years, Larry's strategies of BEP and doing the opposite have proven to be game-changers. Now, I even give lectures!"
—Mick Bowles, PhD Candidate in Construction Management (Australia)

"Larry Stein's brilliant book about his stuttering journey is infused with heartwarming stories of triumph over adversity. He gives hope to many of us who have stuttered all of our lives and didn't think becoming a confident speaker was achievable."
—Ismail Turay Jr., regional editor for major U.S. newspaper company, and US Army officer (USA)

"Larry gets away from techniques and encourages us to have fun speaking. Through our personal meetings, he has shown me and so many others who stutter that not only can we speak with confidence, we can speak like professional speakers."
—Hillel Krief, Data Analyst (Israel)

"I have had the honor to get to know Larry and he has helped me tremendously in becoming a more fluent speaker. This book is a must-read for anyone who has struggled with stuttering, it provides an effective pathway to recovery."

—Jason Zhang, Vice President, Investments (China)

"This book is a true inspiration! It is invaluable to learn how he managed to turn his stuttering and life around. Thank you Larry for sharing your stuttering journey. Your success and desire to share what worked for you with other people who stutter is truly commendable!"

—Dr. Yelena Averbukh, MD, Board Certified Internist (USA)

"I wish I had this book 30 years ago! Larry Stein selflessly lays down an intimate confession of his personal journey, giving hope and detailed strategies to help those of us who stutter improve our speech, change our mindset and lead fulfilling lives."

—Vesna Palaversa, Practitioner of Psychotherapy (Croatia)

My deepest thanks to my:
Family who raised me; you gave me hope.
Family of today; you are my love and my life.
Family of people I mentor; you are my inspiration.

Contents

Introduction: My Biggest Surprise xi

SECTION 1:
The Costs of Compromise 1

SECTION 2:
Relearning to Speak 49

SECTION 3:
Retraining My Brain 75

SECTION 4:
Insights 109

APPENDIX 1:
Roadmap for Improving Your Speech 151

APPENDIX 2:
Answers to Twenty Questions about Stuttering 159

Continue the Conversation 173

Acknowledgments 175

About the Author 179

INTRODUCTION
My Biggest Surprise

EVERY TIME I THINK ABOUT my life, I still can't believe how it has turned out. I did just about everything wrong, and yet, here I am writing a book about how I realized my dreams, and then some.

Why do I tell you this? Because no matter how badly you stutter, no matter how bleak you feel your situation may be, you still have the potential to live your dreams.

Think of it: I hid my stuttering and avoided talking, compromised my career and personal life, suffered terrible depressions, and let stuttering dominate me for decades. I was the stuttering poster child for what not to do.

And yet, here I am.

Now, don't get me wrong; I had a lot of things going for me that many don't have: loving parents and siblings, sufficient resources, a loving wife and kids, good friends, and numerous intangibles. If not for those advantages, I could picture myself living on the street, or worse. I'm well aware of how fortunate I have been. It very easily could have gone the other way. It could have been tragic.

Today, I live a life I could never have imagined. I have a wonderful family and the business of my dreams. Instead of being consumed with stuttering, today it is not a concern; I rarely think about it. I'm a confident speaker, completely comfortable saying what I want. In fact, sometimes I even get paid to speak. I still can't believe it: me, a professional speaker!

But those aren't the biggest surprises of my life. I dreamed about my business, I even dreamed about giving speeches, though neither came easy. But I could never have dreamed that one day I would help others with their speech, and they, aside from my family, would provide the most rewarding experiences of my life.

Even more, I could never imagine how it would feel to speak effortlessly without the stress, struggle, or uncertainty of stuttering. To feel words flow. To relish the joy of conversation, the warmth of connection. It never occurred to me; it wasn't even on my radar. How could I possibly imagine such a life after fifty years of stuttering?

In a life full of surprises, this may be the biggest of them all: that someday I would be free to speak.

Section 1:
The Costs of Compromise

Stuttering Facts

Being part of "the 1 percent" is something that many in America strive for. It suggests that you are in the wealthiest 1 percent of the country; I am not a part of that club. But there is another 1 percent club that I am a part of that many try to disown: the 1 percent of people who stutter.

That's right, it is estimated that 1 percent of Americans stutter, about three million, with a similar percentage around the world. That's one of the few facts I know about stuttering, and frankly, I question whether it's accurate. It seems to be an inflated number since I've hardly met anyone else who stutters, except at stuttering conferences or on stuttering sites. It could be that most people who stutter try to hide it—I certainly did.

Another fact I know about stuttering is that roughly 5 percent of young children stutter and about 80 percent of them "resolve" it by age ten. That's how we get to the 1 percent number. After age ten, good luck, you're probably stuck with it for the rest of your life, though some people improve their speech to varying degrees with therapy and other methods. I'm among the fortunate ones, though I still have my moments now and then. I don't know how many of us there are, but it seems to be a small enough club for a leading researcher on stuttering to call me "an anomaly."

To my knowledge, those are the facts on stuttering, though shockingly few in number and questionable at that. Frankly, the facts never mattered to me. Knowing that I was not alone didn't make speaking any easier or the embarrassment less painful. No matter what others said, however compassionate and heartfelt, I felt cursed—that was the only fact that mattered to me.

My Childhood Wish

My mom walked into the kitchen carrying a cake topped with seven candles. Carefully placing the cake down in front of me, the candles flickering in the dark, she said, "Go ahead, Larry, make a wish."

Did I wish for a new mitt? A new bike? No, those didn't even enter my mind. I'm sure my mom knew what I would wish for and so did the rest of my family at the table. I quietly said to myself, pleading with almost religious fervor, "I wish that I could talk."

That was my wish, for decades on end: I wish that I could talk. All my life, I bounced from wish to wish, hoping that wish would come true. It wouldn't happen for fifty years; the amazing thing is that it happened at all.

I don't remember when I first stuttered. My mom said I didn't talk until the age of four, and right from the start, I spoke in complete sentences. Only after I had my own kids did I realize how strange that must have been to have a child not speak until the age of four. At some point soon thereafter, I must have started stuttering, because I entered kindergarten right around my fifth birthday, and I'm pretty sure I stuttered by then.

The Costs of Compromise

Look through my elementary school pictures, and you'll notice something odd: red, splotchy cold sores under my nose or around the sides of my mouth. That's how stressed I was, even as a young kid. I didn't have to wear my emotions on my sleeve; they were right there under my nose.

Actually, I loved certain parts of school. I was a good student and was blessed with some really close friends. I was also a big kid and one of the best athletes, so sports became my refuge. All in all, I had a pretty good childhood, except for that one fear that always seemed to lurk in the back of my mind and pop up at the worst possible times.

My teacher happily announces, "It's reading time." The mere mention jolts me. Tension kicks in and overtakes me. Like the drip-drip of a water torture, the countdown begins: seven kids to go, six, five, four ... As my turn gets closer, the anxiety builds. By the time it's my turn, I'm in a full panic.

Teeth clenched and head shaking, every word is a struggle. But the outside appearance is nothing compared with the battle raging inside: my mind races, my face fills with heat, and I feel an embarrassment that few will ever know. The reading ends, I'm exhausted, and my jaw hurts. I smile meekly as if to say, "Yeah, I'm okay, no big deal." But it was a big deal, and I knew it would happen tomorrow, the next day, and for way too many tomorrows after that. You may not see my scars from these experiences, but even more than fifty years later, I question if they're fully healed.

Then there was the annual school play. I actually did pretty well with school plays. I always had a few lines and looked forward to them, that is, until fifth grade. Maybe my speech was getting worse or maybe I was becoming more self-conscious. In any case, I had only one line in that year's play, and it turned out to be more than enough.

In the first rehearsal, I said my line with ease, "A square meal it shall be." But my teacher (whom I adored) suggested I say it with a rising pitch at the end. It was a reasonable request, a modest change, and certainly an easy adjustment for most kids.

But for me, it triggered one of the worst periods of anxiety I have ever experienced. For weeks, I struggled to say that line, stuttering terribly on nearly every consonant of the five-word phrase: the "sq" in square, the "m" in meal, the "sh" in shall, and the "b" in be. Not only in class, but even when I practiced by myself in front of a mirror at home. It was so traumatic that I still remember every sound and every stutter more than fifty years later.

No amount of practice helped, whether in school or in the basement of my house. In fact, my stuttering only got worse. The tension grew as the days before the play ticked down. Finally, on the night before the play, I cried hysterically, screaming in my room that I couldn't go on. I threw down my glasses so hard they broke. My mom came in my room and pleaded with me to go on, but she finally gave in and let me stay home. I don't remember ever being so upset in my life.

Sometime later, my mom tried to convince me to join an acting troupe at a local theater. In retrospect, it was a great idea, but I wouldn't give it a thought. I just wasn't ready to take that leap. Speaking was too hard for me. Too bad, it could have helped—Mom had the right idea.

That was my life for as long as I can remember. I could get by on small talk and an occasional cute comment, but anything beyond that was often challenging and sometimes torturous. Even just asking for ketchup at the family dinner table filled me with angst. I found it much easier to speak one on one rather than in front of a group, even if the group was my parents and two older siblings.

Fortunately, I grew up on a small, dead-end street within seven houses of my two best friends in the world, and nearly as close to a few others. We played day and night, usually in the street during the summer and at a friend's house in the winter. It was one game after another—football, baseball, driveway hockey, board games, cards—there was little need for talking. Just walk down the street, knock on their doors, and play all day. My friends on the street saved me.

So did my mom, dad, brother, and sister. They were loving and supportive. In particular, my mom spent countless hours bringing me to speech therapists and encouraging me to keep trying. I cannot imagine how difficult this must have been for her. My father was also very involved; always encouraging, always trying to lift my spirits. As you will read, every member of my family had a part to play in my eventual improvement. I was fortunate that they were a part of my life, especially in the early years. Without the support of my family, my childhood could have been tragic. Then, in my adult years, my wife and kids would save me again. Like I said, I have been very fortunate.

A Religious Experience

The stresses of speaking kept coming, turning many of life's ordinary moments—even religious events—into highly charged, traumatic experiences. Passover is one of the most commonly celebrated holidays on the Jewish calendar. Families get together for a ritual dinner and service called a seder. They read from a book called the Haggadah, sing, and eat a lot.

The seders at my grandparents' house were the stuff of family legend, often including more than thirty people, with wonderful food and old-world, table-pounding songs at the end of the night. I loved those songs and looked forward to singing them every year. Singing was the one thing I could do with my voice without any fear of stuttering. I sang every chance I could, in the shower and in my house, but nothing compared to the singing at our seders.

Then our seders changed. The singing continued, but the seders became a bit more Americanized, moving from an all-Hebrew service chanted mainly by my grandfather to one that included a smattering of English readings. The change was supposed to get the grandchildren more involved. Nice idea for most, but not me: I liked my involvement just the way it was. That one change turned my beloved Passover seders into a terrible source of angst.

Passover takes place in the spring, but not for me—not after the change to English readings at our seders. After that, I always got a head start. By October (six months or so beforehand), fear began to creep into my consciousness. As the months ticked off toward Passover, a sense of dread cast a pall over me as I thought about having to read in front of everyone at the seder. The closer it got to Passover, the more anxious I became. After two torturous years of reading, I knew I couldn't take it anymore. I begged my mom to get me out of reading at the next seder. When that night finally arrived, time passed excruciatingly slowly as I waited to see if I would be called on to read. Once I was sure that I was safe, I was filled with a bewildering mix of relief and embarrassment. Oddly enough, I was okay with that; at least I didn't have to read again.

The Costs of Compromise

One of the most important moments in a young Jewish boy's life is his bar mitzvah, when at the age of thirteen, he reads from the Torah (Hebrew Bible) and Haftarah (prophetic writings), leads some prayers, and gives a speech. Years of Hebrew school and months of study specifically related to the bar mitzvah culminate in this one special day. Most kids focus on the party afterward—that never even entered my mind. I had bigger things to worry about: I would have to talk in front of a large crowd.

My parents did everything possible to reduce the stress of the event. I was originally scheduled for a traditional Saturday morning bar mitzvah, but I would have to share the service with two other boys, and there would be upward of three hundred people there, so my parents moved the service to a Saturday night Mincha to make it easier for me. There would be maybe only a hundred people there, and I wouldn't have to compete with the two boys who spoke fluently. To make it even easier for me, I asked my mom and she agreed to get me out of giving the customary speech; the chanting of the Torah, Haftorah, and prayers would be quite enough. I cannot imagine what would have happened if I had to give a speech.

Picture this: Two nights before my bar mitzvah, I went with my mom to the synagogue for a brief rehearsal. I stood on the bimah (stage) with the two other boys, ready to chant some lines of Hebrew. The first boy read for a minute or two, then the second. Both uneventful, no big deal.

Then, it was my turn. I stood there, ready to go. But I couldn't get a word out. Nothing. I struggled terribly: head shaking, lips pursed, teeth clenched. Just imperceptible sounds of struggle, like I was drowning. I don't know how long I was locked in a death grip up there. It could have been seconds; it could have been minutes; I have no idea. But at some point, someone mercifully pulled me off the bimah. My face flushed with embarrassment, heat rose from my cheeks to my forehead, and I meekly walked down the steps to my mom. For decades, I would know those feelings all too well again and again in other situations. More than fifty years later, I can still feel the heat.

I don't know how my mom handled this moment; I never asked her. But I can't imagine seeing my own son go through such pain. And I can't imagine what was going through her mind, knowing that in just two short nights, her young son would be back up on the very same bimah to do about thirty minutes of reading and chanting (if everything went well) in front of a hundred family members and friends. It seemed like a nightmare waiting to happen. I can't imagine the conversations my parents must have had in the forty-eight hours leading up to that day. I have to think it was much harder on them than on me. As you will soon read, it turned out to be an unforgettable evening.

Failing at the Finest Stuttering Programs

Stuttering dominated me. Consumed me. Even when I wasn't speaking, it was often all I could think about. Stuttering hung over me like an ominous cloud, always threatening to wreck my day. As much as I wished that I could stop stuttering, my mom may have wanted it more. When I was in elementary school, she brought me to the Northwestern University stuttering program, which was known as one of the finest in the country. While my friends played outside on Saturdays, I sat in a room with adults trying to do the one thing I dreaded most: talking.

Maybe I was too young or immature, but I didn't make any headway. In fact, I may have picked up some bad habits from watching other kids stutter, including one unfortunate child who had a particularly violent stutter—he was a lips-pursed, teeth-clenched, head-shaking mess. The first time I met him, I couldn't believe what I was seeing, I felt so bad for him. Soon that became me. I only saw that boy a few times, but it was enough to pick up his unfortunate habits and saddle myself with violent stuttering for decades. The irony was absurd. (Note: There is no scientific evidence that kids in stuttering programs pick up the habits of others who stutter; my personal experience should not dissuade anyone from working with professional therapists—I highly recommend professional treatment.)

At Northwestern, the therapists tried to get me to do voluntary stuttering. The strategy was intended to reduce my sensitivity to stuttering. Now, as an adult, it makes perfect sense: Rather than fear stuttering, do it on purpose. But to an eight-year-old kid struggling to get a word out, it seemed like the craziest thing I had ever heard. They taught me how to "bounce," which is to repeat sounds voluntarily and simply move on to the next word. But it wasn't so simple, at least not for me. When I bounced, I almost always got caught up in a full-blown stuttering block that I couldn't escape.

Still, I did learn some things of value at Northwestern. They introduced me to the idea of phrasing. Instead of having me read a full sentence at one time, they taught me how to read in phrases. Later in my life I would develop my own take on phrasing, but this was an important start.

By my early teens, I was desperate enough to try another well-known program, this time at the University of Chicago (UC). I wrote an impassioned letter to the head of the program, asking for admittance, and got in. Twice a week, my mom and I drove an hour or more each way from the northern suburbs of Chicago to Hyde Park, in the south end of the city. At UC, they gave my mom and me headphones and sat us across from each other in glass booths as we read the play *Our Town*. The headphones had delayed auditory feedback, which enabled me to be pretty fluent. I was told to read by phrasing and pausing in between the phrases, which made a lot of sense to me. This built on my therapy at Northwestern and would become an essential part of my future approach.

I loved being able to speak with my mom and spend large blocks of time with her, but my fluency didn't carry over outside of the booths, even with simple reading. In high school, while my friends were out of town either sunning or skiing during Christmas vacation, I sat alone in our living room, struggling to read aloud. I could barely get out a word. Tears came to my eyes; I remember it like it was yesterday, some fifty years later. UC was the last university stuttering program I would try. I gave up and resolved myself to a life of stuttering.

Could you blame me? Every effort I made to improve my speech ended in miserable failure. When I was young, I was told that maybe I would grow out of it. When that didn't happen, I thought going to speech therapy would cure me. When that didn't happen, I asked my mom to buy me a metronome and a tape recorder; I would cure myself. When that didn't happen, I thought I could get through life without talking much. And while I found that, yes, I could get through life without talking much, it turned out to be not much of a life. I wanted more.

But how could I get there? Nothing I tried got me anywhere. Not therapy, not on my own. Once in a while, someone would give me an article about a new technique or machine that offered promise, but these so-called breakthroughs always had a downside. One machine made you sound like a robot; another technique seemed too ridiculous to try. After a while, these well-intentioned suggestions felt like insults. *Do I give you articles to improve your life? Leave me alone.* Though I would never say that. I had to face it: There were no answers, no widely accepted methods of improvement, no holy grail. It seemed hopeless. There was nothing more to do but give up. And so I did.

My Mind on Stuttering

In recent years, when people learn that I once stuttered heavily, they often mention the movie *The King's Speech*, assuming that my speech was like the portrayal of King George VI. Bad assumption. The truth: not even close. The king in the movie often repeated sounds, hesitated, or spoke haltingly. The movie was celebrated for its raw portrayal of a frustrated stutterer, and it won several Academy Awards.

But frankly, it's another point of resentment: The king's stuttering was nothing like mine. I would have been thrilled to stutter like him. My stuttering was a series of car crashes, one head-on collision after another. Sometimes, I would be locked in a mortal struggle to speak. Stuck in a hard block, I often felt like I was drowning, gasping for my last breaths. Lips pursed, teeth clenched, head shaking, and eyes shut, my jaw would actually ache after conversations. It literally hurt to talk.

Later in life, a dentist was horrified by the sight of my teeth, saying, "You must gnash your teeth terribly in your sleep. You need a mouthguard!" The dentist was a more recent personal friend, and I was too embarrassed to tell him that the condition of my teeth had nothing to do with gnashing in my sleep—it was probably from fifty years of stuttering. I bought the mouthguard and didn't say a word.

I'm sure that some people who once knew me will be surprised to read about my challenges. I probably seemed normal enough on the outside, and I may have been. But there was so much more to my stuttering than what you could see; that was just the tip of the iceberg. Below the surface was pure insanity. My mind raced incessantly like ping-pong balls bouncing frenetically in the glass cases you see in lottery commercials, desperately trying to avoid stuttering on this word, that sound.

Always on red alert for a stutter on the horizon, I would frantically search for a substitute word that I could say more easily and slip seamlessly into a conversation. If I got stalled in my search or couldn't get the new sentence started, I often tossed in filler words, such as umms and uhhs, to get me through. I floundered at the mercy of stuttering, hoping I could make it through a sound, a word, a sentence, a thought, a conversation, a day.

I was an artist at word substitution and filler words; I was also exhausted from it. Anticipating stuttering gobbled up nearly all of my mental bandwidth; I could hardly think of anything else. The calculations were endless, mind-numbing. Sometimes, during an especially long and hard block, the calculations were so consuming that I couldn't remember what I was trying to say or even what the conversation was about. The anticipation cycle dominated me day and night, streaming through my mind at warp speed, overwhelming sense and logic. It was maddening, draining. There was no letup, no rest.

The cycle was insidious. The more I anticipated, the more frenzied my mind became, desperately seeking escape routes from stuttering. Sometimes it was just easier not to talk at all. Sure, sometimes I would feel a momentary high when my word substitution helped me avoid a stutter, but there was a cost to this addiction: the build-up of irrational fears of certain words and sounds.

When I was a kid, adults often told me that my brain moved faster than my mouth. Oddly enough, I took that to be a compliment. *Wow, my brain is amazing, it moves faster than my mouth! I'm so special!* In retrospect, this was utterly ridiculous. My brain wasn't any different from anyone else's; it was just always locked in overdrive, working overtime to keep up with my crazed efforts to avoid stuttering. To substitute words, I had to think five steps ahead, sentence after sentence, day after day.

In truth, word substitution was an exercise in personal sabotage. It was tantamount to telling my brain, "I can't say this word, I give up, get me another." A single sabotage snowballed into greater fear with every moment of anticipation, avoidance, and substitution, amassing fears that plagued me for decades. As brutal as stuttering could be, a bad block was only a single moment in time. Word substitution was like a bully, carrying a lifetime of fear.

That was my existence, holding on for dear life, trying anything to avoid stuttering. As a result, my speech was rigid, hesitant. When I was speaking, smiling was difficult, laughing was nearly impossible. I was always on high alert, trying to anticipate when stuttering might rear its ugly head. And then, when stuttering did strike, I was a sitting duck. One bad block often led to a string of exhausting stutters, maybe for the rest of that conversation, that day, that week, even that month.

So many years of stuttering filled me with destructive tendencies, which I later called inclinations. There seemed to be no end to these stuttering inclinations, many of which were rooted in avoiding stuttering. Avoiding speaking situations and turning down opportunities became my default, go-to response. It was much easier to stick with the status quo and watch the world go by. Avoiding pain in the short term made life much easier, but from a long-term perspective, it was terribly damaging. My life was filled with regrets, depression, and feelings of helplessness. The scars dug deep.

In a sense, I was a prisoner of my own mind. Occasionally, I would enjoy more fluent speech, sometimes for an hour, a day, maybe even a few days in a row. I would become hopeful that maybe this was it, maybe I was done with stuttering. And then, one block would lead to another and another, and splat, there I was, back to square one, back to full-on stuttering. The frustration was terrible; the depression was worse. When I was young, there were long stretches of time in which I barely spoke, sometimes for weeks.

I felt cursed, thinking, *Why me? Why is life so hard for me? Why is it so easy for everyone else?* I had so much to say, but I couldn't. I knew I could do more, be more, but speaking was too often a pitched battle, an overwhelming struggle. Sometimes I just wasn't up for a fight and kept quiet, resigned to frustration. The other 330 million people in America had fun talking, chatting away at parties, telling jokes, and speaking effortlessly on the phone. Looking at them, it seemed so easy, so natural. *Why couldn't I do that?*

The Costs of Compromise

Why do I have to be different? I was about twenty-five when my older brother, Marty, came into town from California for a family event. We were seated in rows, and he sat in the row directly in front of me and my friend, who had begun talking with me. Then my brother did the impossible: He turned around toward us, smiled warmly, and casually introduced himself to my friend. Like it was nothing! Like he was happy to meet the guy! How was that even possible? In all my years, I had never introduced myself, at least not willingly. And my brother did it with a casual smile, like it was nothing! Like he enjoyed it! And I'm sure he did. *Why couldn't I do that?*

Introducing myself was the stuff of nightmares (which I still have). Fortunately, I figured out a way to get through it: Just avoid meeting new people. Or hide behind my parents, siblings, wife, kids, or anyone else I could. Or just walk the other way. Anything to not say my name. But there was a cost to my hiding: I lost out on a lot of life. Sure, I had regrets, but I had less pain. In those days, I thought the trade-off was worth it; now I don't. In retrospect, I know that avoiding social situations caused me to miss out on a lot of good times and a number of relationships that could have been fun and rewarding.

I'm sure that I was often viewed as standoffish and unfriendly in my college days and in my twenties and thirties, when really, I was just too uncomfortable to become part of the gang. It's not that I didn't want to fit in—I couldn't fit in. I couldn't speak in groups, the glare of everyone's eyes was too much for me; I would freeze and struggle to speak. I wish I had another shot at those relationships, but after so many years, I doubt that I ever will—they're lost. It's a regret I have to live with. As difficult as it was for me to be part of a group, there was one speaking situation that was even more challenging and much more painful. It dogged me relentlessly and, despite my prodigious, almost comical efforts to avoid it, sometimes I just couldn't.

Fear of Phone

The phone terrorized me. I'm not alone; just about every person I've met who stutters feels the same way. Just the shrill ring alone was enough to jolt me. It was one terrifying moment after another: fear, panic, blocking to the max. It was brutal.

Today's phone experience is a completely different animal, a much kinder one at that. Now we have personal cell phones with caller ID and voicemail. I can set my own ring and even make it a fun song; nothing like the shrill ring of my youth. I don't even have to answer the phone; I can let it go to voicemail. Better yet, I almost always know who is calling. What a beautiful world! That technology would have made my life so much easier years ago.

Phones were much more challenging when I was growing up in the 1960s and '70s. There was no caller ID, so you didn't know who was calling—you didn't know if it was your friend, your parents' friend, or a complete stranger. There were no robocalls or spam calls. Every call was real, and since there was no voicemail, you had to answer every call—you didn't have a choice. And that was a problem: I didn't have a choice—I had to answer every call. Not having a choice creates nightmares for those of us who stutter; we always need an out in case we have trouble talking. There was an implicit contract in those days:

The Costs of Compromise

You had to answer the phone. No exceptions. Absolute nightmare.

At first, when I was deemed old enough to answer the phone, I did so with a casual "Hello." That didn't last long. One day, that casual "Hello" became not so casual; it wouldn't come out. I was stuck. I panicked and came up with a substitute word. Instead, I answered the phone with "Yes." And it worked! "Yes" worked! For a while. Then "Yes" became my new nightmare. I couldn't get past the "Y," and I couldn't come up with another substitute. It was terribly embarrassing, struggling to answer the phone in front of my family. Worse yet, it was an embarrassment I couldn't avoid—I had to answer the phone.

From that point on, even my own house became a source of angst. When my family was home, I tried to position myself between the phone in the kitchen and the phone in the back of our family room. If I were exactly in the middle of those two phones, there would almost always be someone closer. Almost always. There were times when I had to answer the phone, and it wasn't pretty. Each failed answer of the phone made me more desperate to avoid it. The mental machinations to avoid answering the phone became exhausting. No place was safe, even in my own house!

The same went for my dad's men's clothing store, which otherwise was a godsend in many ways. I really liked working at his store. I got to be with my dad, and waiting on customers proved to be great therapy for my stuttering. In fact, working at the store was the first time that I "played" with my speech. I probably got the idea from watching my dad, who always had fun with his customers. He played, so I played. This was new for me. It also helped that his store was forty miles away from our house. I felt so free, being away from home where no one knew me. I recall thinking, *No one knows me here let's just enjoy this!* So, I became a completely different person at the store and played with my speech. As long as I played with my speech and focused on having fun, I stuttered only occasionally, which was a great release and confidence-builder for me. Decades later, I would draw on this experience to play with my speech, which would have a profound effect on me. Thanks, Dad.

There was just one problem with the store: It had two phones on the main floor and one phone in the basement. Through high school and occasionally during breaks in college, I worked in the basement, which had clothing for teens and college kids. That was safe because with only one phone, I could easily position myself far away from it so others would answer it. But during the relatively few times that I worked on the main floor, life became a bit more treacherous. Fortunately, I had a plan for that. With two phones, one on either end, I positioned myself exactly in the middle of the floor in hopes there would always be someone else closer to the phone. And there was.

Except once. Just once in all those years, but I will never forget it. I was probably about twenty years old, and I happened to be walking upstairs to the main floor. No one else was around, except my dad, who was way in the back. In a stroke of horrible luck, the phone rang just as I passed by. The ring jolted me, I fell into an instant panic. I knew what I had to do; there was no way around it. I screwed on my courage and answered by saying the name of the store as everyone else did, but not quite: Mmmmmmmmmmmmmmmmmr. Fffffffffffffffffloyd's.

I don't know how long that block took; it seemed like hours, maybe days. The caller asked for my dad. When my dad answered the phone, I don't know what the caller said, but judging from my dad's response, I'm pretty sure the caller asked something like, "Who was that?" I can still feel the heat rising in my face from the embarrassment.

I'm sure my dad was embarrassed, too, though we never talked about it. As I am writing this, some forty-five years later, I can still feel my face flush with embarrassment, I can still feel the heat.

The Happiest Place on Earth

Disneyland is known as the happiest place on earth. But not for one sixteen-year-old boy on one particular day. It should have been. I grew up hearing so much about Disneyland and how everyone loved it. In particular, I couldn't wait to see the TV studio. After all, it was 1972, long before movie theme parks were created, so this was one of the most popular attractions at Disneyland.

My family and I walked into the set of *McHale's Navy*, one of my favorite TV shows. I couldn't believe that I was looking at the bridge that actors Ernest Borgnine and Tim Conway made famous, exchanging one-liners and hatching crazy schemes. I loved that show. *Wow, wouldn't it be great to stand on that bridge!*

Then it happened. The tour leader said, "I'm looking for two people to be our actors for *McHale's Navy*. Any volunteers?"

When no one volunteered, he told the crowd, "Hmmm, I'm looking for two people who are doing their best to hide from me."

Within seconds, he chose a thin, bouncy woman in her forties. She happily took her place on the bridge next to him, giddy with excitement.

Then, scanning the room again, his eyes slowly approached my side of the room. I could feel the tension rising, my mind racing with fear, *Oh no, not me. Keep going, not me.*

He scanned the side, back and forth, then reached out his hand toward me and called out, "You!"

I couldn't believe it. "Me?"

He nodded with a big smile. "Yes, you, come on down!"

Oh God, why me? I shrieked silently. My mind shifted into overdrive, racing at hyper-speed. Panic engulfed me as I walked reluctantly to the bridge.

The tour leader turned to the woman next to me, and she happily gave her name and hometown, smiling all the way. Then he swung the microphone toward me. Big mistake; he had no idea what he was in for. I'm sure he quit his job later that day.

I knew what was coming, and there was nothing I could do about it. He was going to ask THE question, the one I feared most. And I would have to answer him, in front of everyone and, worse yet, in front of my family.

"And your name?"

"Lllllllllllllllllllllllllarrrry Stststststst——ein."

It seemed to take minutes, hours, I don't know. The room fell silent. My face broke out into a full sweat.

Stunned, the leader hesitated before asking his next question, as if he were wondering whether it was worth it. He inquired gently, "And where are you from?"

I actually felt better about this question. I could usually rely on the "sh" sound. I replied, "Sshh, Chicago."

Phew, got through that one! I was really from Highland Park, a suburb twenty-five miles north of Chicago, but hey, close enough.

Who's going to know!

I prayed that he wouldn't ask anything else, and he didn't. I got to act as if I were driving the boat, feel the mechanical waves, and, best of all, get the hell out of there. So much for childhood dreams. Decades later, I would go to Disney World with my own kids. I didn't enjoy it much; I wonder why? We only went that one time and never went back.

Reality Strikes

By my senior year in high school, my future stared me right between the eyes. Until then, I could get by playing sports for the high school teams and with my friends, but those days were numbered; I had to face the reality of becoming an adult. What kind of work could I possibly do with my stuttering? I guess I could have kept working at my dad's store. But I had my own dreams and wanted my own life.

But what life? Sure, I could make small talk and cute comments. I could enjoy being with friends. But go beyond small talk or place me in a challenging situation, and stuttering would overwhelm me. I couldn't have a conversation of any length or meaning without falling into stuttering, often severe. I kept coming back to the same question: What kind of work could I possibly do?

Fortunately, I was one of those kids who knew exactly what he wanted to do with his life. From the time I was eleven, I was hooked on the stock market. This was another influence from my dad. After dinner, he would settle into his big yellow chair in the corner of our living room, with *The Chicago Daily News* opened wide. One night, I finally asked what he was reading. He suggested that I walk around to the back of his chair and take a look. It felt like I was peeking behind the Wizard's curtain. I was fascinated, mesmerized: full-length newspaper pages of tiny numbers neatly arranged in long columns. I asked him what it was, he told me, and so began my lifelong obsession with the stock market.

My dad and I talked on and on about it. He encouraged me to research the markets and read books on the subject. By eighth grade, I was reading *Business Week* cover to cover. After football practice, I would ride my bike to the Highland Park Library, pore through Value Line reports, and read every book I could find on the stock market. By the time I graduated from high school, I had read just about every book on investing in the Highland Park Library, though I must admit there weren't many in those days.

I started investing at age thirteen with the money from my bar mitzvah. I got lucky on my first investment, Champion Home Builders. The stock rose an astounding 130 percent in six months! I would love to tell you that I came up with the idea, but in truth, I read about it in one of my dad's stock market magazines. Still, at that age, I thought it was my own brilliant idea (it wasn't), and I was hooked. Even on family vacations, I would bring my stock market books and reading materials. Investing was my passion, my love—even more than football. I couldn't get enough of it. Until reality set in.

During my senior year of high school, the future was no longer a wistful dream in the distance; it was here, now. I knew what I wanted to do; I wanted to be in the investment field. So, at my dad's suggestion, I got dressed up in a suit and tie and went downtown to speak with my dad's broker (mine, too) about making it a career.

The Costs of Compromise

The broker said, "Sure, you can make it a career. But all of the jobs here in Chicago are in sales. Is that what you want? To sell?" I shook my head, dejectedly. I knew I couldn't sell; I could barely ask him the question. He continued, "You can be an analyst, but all the analyst jobs are in New York. Do you want to go to New York?" Again, I shook my head no. How could I make it in New York by myself? I couldn't even ask for directions to get there. And that was the end of it. My dream was dashed, done, gone in five minutes.

But it shouldn't have been. Other kids so dedicated to a dream wouldn't have stopped there. They would have networked with other professionals in the field and learned that there was, in fact, a small but growing investment analyst community in Chicago. Or they would have planned their college studies to set themselves up for an investment analyst career in New York. Or they would have dedicated themselves to improving their speech. I did none of those. I didn't ask a question; I didn't make a call. I folded. What else could I do? I was deathly afraid of the phone, and introducing myself was even worse. What was I to do with my stuttering? What kind of work could I possibly do?

"Son, have you thought about accounting?" my dad asked. It was a beautiful summer day. The wind whisked through our hair as we drove to my dad's store in his old convertible.

"You're good with numbers, and maybe you won't have to talk so much. It's a good career. There's always a need for accountants. You could always get a job."

That was all I needed to hear. Finally, I had something to do. It wasn't my dream, but it was something to do, something I could do. Two months later, I went downstate to the University of Illinois for my freshman year and enrolled as an accounting major—whatever that was. It's true, I had no idea what accounting was or what an accountant did. But I thought I wouldn't have to talk much, and that was good enough for me.

My Grand Compromise

The choice to major in accounting marked the start of my grand compromise: giving up my dreams to enter a field I didn't even know—all to avoid stuttering. I soon learned what accounting was, and frankly, it didn't interest me at all. Nothing did. I hated school. I went to the library every night and stared at my books, seeing no purpose in what I was doing. I was at the wrong school in the wrong curriculum, and I did nothing about it.

My heart was still with investing, but that door was closed (only because I closed it). So, I made my grand compromise to be an accountant. It was so depressing that I couldn't focus on accounting or any other subject. Ironically, one of the first topics discussed in Psych 100 during my first semester of college was cognitive dissonance, which is when a person experiences psychological stress by doing something against their beliefs. I didn't need to learn about cognitive dissonance; I was living it. I would soon become an expert, exhibit A in the textbook.

I loved writing, and I loved the stock market, but in college, I did neither except for an advanced-level writing class that was disappointing enough to keep me from taking another. I drank too much, studied too little, and spent most of my time angry with my life. Night after night, I would say to myself in frustration, *Time is passing, and I am not.*

Drinking became a release for me. I knew I was wasting my life, but I couldn't see a way out. What else could I do with my stuttering? So, I drank myself into oblivion several nights a week, sometimes to the point of vomiting. Hanging out in the bars gave me something of a social life. It was easier to talk when I was drunk, and no one could hear me anyway above the loud music. In the bars, I felt much less inhibited with my speech, nearly normal, almost cool.

In retrospect, drinking was easy and comfortable, but it led to a downward spiral. Formerly an A student, I descended deeper and deeper into the muck. I took tests with barely any preparation, usually only studying at the last moment. For decades after college, I had nightmares about not being able to find my books with a test just a few hours away. Forty-five years later, I think those nightmares have finally come to an end. I think.

College wasn't a total loss. I made some friends, dated some nice girls, and had some fun. And I did one thing right: I met my wife, Susan. I felt an easy calm with her, we could talk for hours—I could actually talk! We met my senior year when we moved into apartments that were nearly adjoining. During the first semester, we developed a wonderful friendship. Feeling a new sense of security, my drinking soon came to a stop. I was changing, maturing. Our friendship turned to dating early in the second semester, and four years later, we got married. She saved my life then, and she would save it again years later.

As I implied a bit earlier about Susan: I felt so comfortable with her that I rarely ever stuttered. Early in our relationship, a friend of hers had to do a video project for a class, and she needed a narrator.

Susan suggested, "Why don't you use Larry? He has a nice voice." Her friend laughed and said, "Are you kidding? He stutters!" I think that was the first time Susan learned of my little secret. She only recently learned about another secret: I couldn't say her name, so I made up a bunch of nicknames. Those nicknames have stuck for more than forty-five years, and they're not going away anytime soon, even though I can now say her name just fine.

I graduated with a BS in accountancy (volumes of truth in that statement), went on for a master's in taxation at DePaul University in Chicago, eventually passed the CPA exam, and got a job as a tax specialist at a major accounting firm, Alexander Grant. I looked great on paper, but it was a sham. I really didn't know much, and I had absolutely no interest in what I was doing. I soon learned that working in accounting was even more boring than studying it. Accounting was great for some of my friends, but it didn't fit me, though it's certainly possible that nothing would have fit me at that stage of my life.

I left Alexander Grant after eighteen months. During the last several months at Grant, I looked feverishly for an opportunity in the investment field and finally found a job at a tiny brokerage firm. It would pay me 20 percent less than my CPA job, but it was worth it: anything to get a shot at the investment world. I loved being in the investment environment, but during the first year, I really wasn't doing anything other than shadowing the firm's founder. He liked having a protégé at his side, a young buddy, but the job was more about socializing with clients and prospects than it was about investing.

It was fun, but eventually, reality set in: To have any value, I would have to bring in clients and generate sales. My speech had improved tremendously over the months, but it was all small talk. The moment I tried to contact prospects to get clients, I couldn't get a word out. I couldn't even make a phone call. It was devastating. I developed heart palpitations, couldn't sleep, and flirted with depression. Another door was closing on me.

Now what? I needed a way to stay in the investment business without having to talk. The answer came quickly. I figured: I live in Chicago, the home of a major options exchange, why don't I trade options? I had saved some money and opened an account at a firm where I could trade options in their office, simply by making phone calls down to the trading floor. I was a bit shaky in my first few calls but soon became comfortable enough with the guys on the phone to make my stuttering a non-issue. This could work!

Things went pretty well in the beginning until the firm tripled its trading costs for off-the-floor traders, squeezing my profitability. With limited funds and not nearly enough knowledge, I felt the pressure of the increased trading costs and soon closed up the business. That led me to think about going downstairs to trade on the actual Chicago Board of Options Exchange trading floor. If I could trade the S&P 500 upstairs over the phone, why couldn't I trade the S&Ps downstairs on the floor at a fraction of the cost?

I soon learned why. I could not have imagined the S&P 500 trading pit: it was pure chaos. At the time, I was six foot one and about 215 pounds. I had never been intimidated on the football field; I always felt invincible. Somehow, this was different. The action was frenzied: a mosh pit of unusually tall men, aggressively shouting orders, their fingers flickering trading signals. I was totally overwhelmed. Heat filled my face, I thought I was going to faint. I lasted less than ten minutes. That's when I knew the trading dream was over—another one down the drain. I couldn't trade upstairs, and I certainly couldn't trade downstairs. Giving up trading was terribly painful, but it was the right thing to do. By now, I was married, and we couldn't risk any more of our nest egg.

I didn't know what to do. I didn't know what I could do. Frustration mounted. Depression began to set in. Doors were closing, and I didn't see any opportunities open to me. Months later, I called my cousin who worked at Deloitte, got an interview, and then a job as a CPA tax specialist. Again, I tried, I really did, but I just didn't fit into the accounting world. I didn't like the work and had little interest in the subject. I lasted eighteen months, and that was it: the end of my accounting career. What a career it was, done and gone at age twenty-seven. Accounting certainly wasn't a dream of mine, but it still marked another loss, and I felt it.

I was running out of options. I had already bombed out in two careers—the one of my dreams and the one of my compromise. I sank into a terrible depression. I couldn't eat, couldn't sleep, couldn't think. I could barely get out of bed, and even then, I struggled to make it to the couch. Smiling was difficult, socializing was painful; I avoided it at all costs. I couldn't see a way out. Nothing seemed possible for me. Every door I could think of was slammed shut. Hope was fading away. I was lost.

Not knowing what to do, I tried once again to revive my dream of investing. I started writing an investment newsletter and wrote an investment book as stepping stones to building my own investment management business. Writing about investing seemed to be the perfect mix of my investment knowledge and writing ability, and better yet, I wouldn't have to talk.

The newsletter grew for a while, but not nearly to the level of subscriptions needed to make a living. A few years later, I published my book with a large New York publisher, John Wiley & Sons. I was thirty-one and on top of the world (for a week), bursting with pride at seeing my book featured in the front windows of Chicago's largest bookstores. The very next week, on October 19, 1987, the stock market crashed. The Dow Jones Industrial Average plunged nearly 23 percent, the largest percentage drop in history for a single day, even much larger than any one-day decline during the 1929 Depression. Incredible timing. Still, with the widespread buzz around the stock market, I thought my book could sell if it was aggressively marketed.

When I contacted the publisher to ask when my book tour would start, they said in the nicest way possible that they didn't think it would be a worthwhile endeavor. I didn't have to ask; I knew why. My speech on the phone call said all there was to know: How could they sponsor a book tour for a guy who couldn't talk?

Still, I was able to talk well enough to call around on my own and get some media quotes with large newspapers such as the *Chicago Tribune*, *Chicago Sun-Times*, *USA Today*, and *Barron's*. But those only went so far. To sell books, I would have to get out there and give presentations, and even my publisher wouldn't support that effort. Sales were disappointing, and the thrill of seeing my book in the windows of major bookstores soon wore off. Reality was setting in again.

Trying to keep the investment dream alive, I earned some money consulting with two large investment firms, though I knew neither of these had any long-term future. I took one last shot at trying to launch my own investment firm. As part of a trip to Los Angeles to visit my brother, one of my oldest and closest friends kindly arranged a meeting with his boss, a well-placed attorney who I thought could introduce me to his wealthy client base.

The boss was nice enough to take the meeting and was gracious throughout. I thought the meeting went reasonably well. But afterward, I got a call from my friend. He was shocked at how badly I stuttered during the meeting. He was flabbergasted, finding it hard to express his surprise (and in my mind, his disappointment). But that's how it was with my stuttering. Through more than twenty years of close friendship, from early childhood on, I was able to fool him with my speech by sticking with small talk and one-liners. Sure, he knew I stuttered, but he had no idea how severe it was until that meeting.

During the meeting, my speech was actually better than in most of my business conversations. I only had a few heavy blocks, but my speech was choppy, mired by hesitations and minor repetitions. I was holding on too tight, trying not to stutter. I got most of my points across, but my speech was labored and uneasy, occasionally to the point of being painful.

Even after the meeting, my friend's boss was kind enough to occasionally take my calls, but eventually, I caught on to the reality that nothing was ever going to happen. I can't blame the failure of impressing his boss entirely on my speech; in truth, I lacked the investment expertise and experience to handle a sophisticated client base. The truth often got lost in the fog of my stuttering.

The Costs of Compromise

Each compromise I made reinforced what I now call the victim mindset, which dominated me throughout my teens and twenties. I didn't consciously choose to be a victim, but in truth, I played the victim day and night. I thought like a victim, acted like a victim, and lived like a victim. So, I guess I was a victim.

In my victim mindset, I thought stuttering was something that happened to me. I had bad stuttering days and good stuttering days, and I referred to them in exactly those ways. I always suspected that a block was right around the corner, just waiting to pounce on me. Maybe this sound, that word, perhaps the next sentence. It was only a matter of time. And all I could do was sit there, wait for it, and take it, like a sitting duck.

In a sense, the victim mindset worked for me, giving me an obvious excuse that everyone could see (and hear) as to why my life was such a disappointment. Given my speech, wasn't it obvious why I stuck with a college major and a career that didn't require much talking, even though it didn't interest me in the least? Doesn't it explain why I wasn't more persistent in pursuing my dreams in the investment field, a career that would probably require me to speak more effectively? These compromises made sense, didn't they?

The excuses mounted and so did the frustration. In the meantime, I saw life passing me by, along with loads of missed opportunities, both in my career and personal life. The excuses may have pacified me for a while, but the truth still gnawed at me. Nothing good ever came out of my victim mindset, which often left me down and sometimes depressed. It was a ticket to nowhere.

Reality was setting in again. My dreams of making it in the investment field were dashed. I had failed on every front I could think of: sales, trading, consulting, newsletter, book, you name it. There was nothing left to try. The dream was done, gone.

Running out of options, I kept hope alive with desperate stabs at rose-colored dreams. I took a shot at becoming a screenwriter. I read books, studied screenplays, wrote a couple, and sent them out to agents. But that didn't go anywhere, either. I had run out of dreams. The only thing left was reality, and it looked terribly grim.

Everywhere I looked, doors were closing. I was married with a child, thirty-one years old, with a string of failures spread out like debris on an empty highway. I had nowhere to go. Who would want to hire a guy who couldn't talk and failed everywhere he went?

Frustration mounted. What could I do? On paper, I was trained for accounting, but that wasn't going to work, I knew that. I desperately wanted to be in the investment field, but I had already crapped out on every front. Sometimes, I walked the streets in desperation, looking at others, wondering, "What do they do? How did they get their job?" Other times, I walked to Lake Michigan and stared out at the water, but there were no answers there, either. Depression set in again.

Finding My Footing

Fortunately, my wife hung in there with me. Not many women would have done so. Susan worked the entire time to keep us afloat financially, including the years when I was depressed and took desperate stabs at various careers. Our first child, Joe, was truly the light of my life; he and Susan saved me. I loved him so much; fatherhood helped pull me out of this depression.

My parents and siblings were also supportive. My sister, Sheri, suggested, "Take one step forward with your life, just one." Maybe it was the right time, the right message, or the right messenger, but somehow that was the nudge I needed. In retrospect, it may have also been the seed idea for a strategy that would later change my life. Thanks, Sher!

I took that one step and started to look through the *Chicago Tribune* job ads. Fortunately, I looked at them on the right day and found a few jobs in a field called investor relations. I didn't know much about investor relations, but it sounded like a good combination of my investment knowledge and writing skills. One of those openings was with NICOR, a large, publicly held natural gas utility. At age thirty-two, I had a fresh start.

The NICOR post saved me. It was a low-pressure job that got me back on my feet. I liked the work: writing investment analyst speeches, annual reports, and press releases. Best of all, I often worked with the chairman and CEO, an understated, classy gentleman named Dick Cline. He took a personal interest in me and taught me a lot. Dick was one of the most respected CEOs in the country and probably one of the kindest, too. Pure class.

I knew that I didn't have a future at NICOR, but I had a present, and that was good enough for now. The NICOR job gave me stability. We bought a house and had our second child, Aaron. Having two sons was a blast. Words cannot describe how much I loved my boys; we played day and night. With one son, I had the little brother I never had; I couldn't imagine anything better. I was wrong. With two sons, it was a different feeling entirely: now we had a family, and I loved it even more.

After my five years at NICOR, Dick Cline decided to retire. I knew that was my cue to leave, too. It was time. It was obvious that my NICOR life would change with a new CEO. Besides, the job had become repetitive. But I got what I needed. For the first time in my life, I had something to build on, the beginnings of a career. Working at NICOR also gave me casual opportunities to speak with coworkers and senior executives. The more I talked, the more comfortable I became. My speech improved quite a bit, not from any therapy or speaking strategy, just from frequently engaging with others and from getting reps.

I was now comfortable with small talk in easy situations and could enjoy carrying on light conversations. When I was young, my father urged me, "Just get out there and talk." Unwittingly, I was finally following his sage advice. While it seemed like I wasn't stuttering much, I really wasn't free—I was still hesitant to speak, often changing my words to make it through a sentence without stuttering. Sometimes, I simply chose not to speak at all. Fortunately, my next job would catapult me into a host of new speaking opportunities, though it almost didn't happen.

The Costs of Compromise

Giving In to Opportunity

I found a position advertised in *The Wall Street Journal* for an investor relations consultant at The Financial Relations Board (FRB). I had heard of the firm and its well-known founder and chairman, Ted Pincus. He was often in the media and was viewed by many as the Chicago authority on investor relations. It seemed like the perfect opportunity. Now at age thirty-seven, with my NICOR position lending some experience as well as a bit more confidence in my speech, I thought I was ready to handle a more challenging work environment. The interview consisted of an impossibly long writing test and a surprisingly brief discussion that was short enough to largely enable me to hide my stuttering. I felt confident about how I did on the writing test, and I thought the interview went well enough to give me a chance at the job.

Later that night, at 9:40 p.m., I received a call that I will never forget: Ted Pincus called to offer me a job. I was stunned and flattered that he would call me personally; even more so because it was late at night. Years later, I learned that's when he made all of his job offers; apparently, he wanted you to feel exactly like I did. Ted congratulated me on doing so well on the writing test. Then he launched into a full description of the job, his scratchy voice brimming with enthusiasm. The more he spoke, the more I thought, I can't do this job. How can I consult with CEOs and CFOs of publicly held companies? How can I tell them what to do? I was thirty-seven years old and had never even told a secretary what to do, much less a CEO. Sure, I had worked with Dick Cline, a highly respected CEO of national repute, but how many

Dick Clines are there in the world who are so kind, compassionate, and understanding?

When Ted finished his description, he said, "So, does this sound like something you would like to do?"

I replied, "Sure, but ..." Reality set in. "I don't think I could do it."

"Why not?"

I thought long and hard about how to phrase my reply in the nicest way possible with words I could say without stuttering. "Well, I have a speech problem."

Ted responded immediately, "Yes, I know. But you'll be good at this. I've seen your writing. Sure, you may have some challenges in the beginning, but once clients get to know you, they'll like your work, and it won't be a problem. You'll see. Think about it overnight and give me an answer in the morning."

The offer was for 50 percent more than I was currently making, with opportunities for further upside. The firm seemed prestigious. Several members of the staff were former newspaper writers from the *Chicago Tribune* and *Chicago Sun-Times*, some of whom I recognized from their bylines, including the one who interviewed me. It was the first job offer I ever received that I felt had long-term potential. I could do this job; I could make it a career, maybe even a lucrative one. Anyone else in my shoes would have jumped at the offer, especially given the raise and financial upside. There was another persuasive factor: I didn't have any other opportunities. I had a wife, two young kids, and a relatively new house—money was an issue.

Even so, my initial inclination was to decline the offer. How could I take the job? Wasn't I setting myself up for failure? Wouldn't my stuttering get in the way? At NICOR, I could simply walk down the hall to give my thoughts to the CEO; at FRB, I would have to call client

The Costs of Compromise

CEOs on the phone. The phone! I've never done that! Would I be able to get a word out, much less an intelligent thought? How long would it take Ted Pincus to realize he made a terrible mistake? A week? A day?

On the other hand, I didn't have another job offer and doubted that I could get one. Frankly, I needed the money. I discussed it with my wife, then tossed and turned about it overnight. I went to sleep that night planning to decline the offer, and woke up with a completely different answer. Maybe it was desperation or a leap of faith, but I finally said yes.

Ted was right. I did have problems speaking with clients in the beginning, but they liked my work, and my stuttering was never really an issue. More importantly, the FRB job pushed me into speaking situations I had never experienced: conversations with colleagues, phone calls with clients, and meetings with groups of professionals—even taking the lead in some meetings. For the first time in my life, I was talking through much of the workday. Speaking was no longer an event; it was an essential part of my day. It was just something I did in the course of my job. This was huge, a sea-change in perspective that had an incredibly positive impact on my speech.

With so much talking on a daily basis, my stuttering defenses were being worn down. Barriers were breaking, and I was becoming more and more comfortable with my speech. For the first time in my life, I advanced beyond small talk and cute quips—I was asking questions and having real conversations, though still stuttering now and then. You might say, "Well, it's about time, you were nearly forty." But I would say, "At least I got there."

Still, I didn't feel comfortable speaking in more challenging situations. I was still holding on too tight, trying not to stutter. At age forty, I collaborated on a program for my synagogue that was perhaps the signature achievement of my life to date. I wrote the opening speech to kick off the event, but I ended up asking a friend to deliver it—I just couldn't do it. As it turned out, we had over a thousand people at the event. Looking around the room, I reminded myself that I wasn't ready for such a pressured speaking situation, though I really wished I could. Sure, I was making progress, but I still lived at the mercy of stuttering. Whether it was calling a stranger, introducing myself, or any number of other difficult speaking situations, I was still filled with fear and stuttered severely or simply avoided the moment entirely. Avoidance was still my first inclination.

Working at FRB was a huge step forward for my career, too. For the first time in my life, I enjoyed a bit of business and financial success. But after about ten years at FRB, the firm began to undergo major changes. Ted retired, he sold the firm, and the new management team didn't appreciate my strengths. The firm was disintegrating right before my eyes. Employees were leaving in droves, and there was almost no one left. The upside had ended; I had to find something new.

Fortunately, a new opportunity arose that would change my life forever. A friend told me about a job possibility with his cousin's financial services firm. Largely focused on insurance, they were thinking of starting an investment arm. He got me an interview, and I hit it off with his cousin. I was forty-seven and thought I was finally ready to handle it from a speaking standpoint. I would earn less than half of what I did at FRB, but I thought it was worth the risk—I was finally back in the investment field! I stayed for five years and learned a lot during that time, particularly about handling clients. Equally important, I became exposed to a new range of speaking situations, which led to another significant leap in my speech.

THE COSTS OF COMPROMISE

GOING AGAINST MY INCLINATION

The investment job wasn't the only reason my speech improved so much; another new opportunity to speak emerged. But once again, it almost didn't happen. My cousin asked me to join the board of a small nonprofit organization where she served as the director of one of its main programs. I joined the board, and a few years later, they asked me to become the volunteer president.

I was stunned, surprised, and, more than that, incredibly flattered. Then my stuttering inclination kicked in with my usual default response: "No thanks." Who was I kidding? No way could I do this. I would have to lead board meetings of twenty people or more, and I had never led a meeting with more than a few. Worse yet, I would have to give brief speeches now and then, usually about five to ten minutes in length, which was something I hadn't done in decades. The last speech I gave was twenty-five years before at Deloitte: a ten-minute talk that took twenty-eight minutes to deliver—that's how badly I stuttered. It was a humiliation that I never wanted to re-live.

The board asked me a few times, and I turned them down a few times, then I finally gave in. Just like taking the job at FRB, this was another time when going against my inclination of saying no would prove to be the right move. Ironically, the two reasons I kept saying no to taking the post—leading board meetings and doing occasional speeches—became the springboards to a realization that would change my life forever.

I struggled quite a bit in the early board meetings, switching out words to avoid stuttering and speaking haltingly at times. But as I became more comfortable with my role, the struggles gradually decreased and my speech improved significantly. I enjoyed being the leader of an organization, however small, and loved brainstorming new ideas with my cousin.

Giving speeches became the launching pad for major improvements in my speech and how I handled challenging speaking situations. I remember my first speech, a little five-minute talk at a fundraising event. My wife and I had arrived early at the event and mingled a bit. Fifteen minutes before the speeches started, I rushed to the washroom to calm myself down. My stomach was twisting and turning, and I was shaky. I kept an eye on my watch to make sure that I wouldn't miss my slot to speak, but frankly, I wasn't ready.

I was introduced to the audience, rose to the podium, and looked out at a crowd of about 150. I knew this feeling, and I knew how it would play out. Even if I were only talking in a group of five, I would feel the glare of a thousand spotlights beating down on me, propelling me into a panic. Helpless, bewildered, I would melt into a hot mess. With 150, it would be worse. This is what I dreaded; this is why I turned down the post so many times.

But then something different happened. As I scanned the crowd, I saw a friend on the right side, flashing a reassuring smile just when I needed it. Basking in her warmth, I saw my cousin in the middle and my wife on the left, and felt their warmth, too. That's what I needed, and my nervousness began to melt. I started talking, basking in their warmth, spurred on by their love. I was no longer speaking to 150; I was speaking to three, and I felt they were all cheering me on. It was a dream come true. My speech wasn't perfect, but I loved the experience and couldn't wait to do another one. I was hooked.

More speeches led to more strategies on how to deal with my

anxiety. To keep myself from getting caught up in the pressure, I would play with the crowd. Humor became my release, interjecting cute, off-hand comments to loosen up the crowd and, more importantly, myself. Instead of folding under the pressure of an audience, I began to feel empowered by their presence. They became my strength.

This led me to try more mind games. My favorite game was pausing for effect after making a point to see how long I could hold the audience in silence before they became fidgety. I took particular delight in doing this, effectively thumbing my nose at the classic stuttering fear of time pressure. In a sense, I was breaking the rules of stuttering, doing the opposite of what I would ordinarily fall prey to. I would pause and hold that pause, and when I saw a few people get uncomfortable, I would start speaking again. It became a game of dare, seeing how far I could push this envelope. I didn't realize this game would one day become the model for one of the most profound speaking strategies I would ever employ.

Public speaking also led me to use a technique I learned in speech therapy: phrasing. I never had any success with phrasing outside of therapy, so I never really used it. For thirty-five years, phrasing laid dormant in my mind. But somehow, when I was doing public speaking for the nonprofit, whether onstage or leading board meetings, I fell into phrasing, and it helped me through.

The improvement in my speech was exciting, empowering me to be more bold with my career. The investment job at the financial services company was an important first step in the right direction, but the cut in my earnings was a constant frustration, and it wasn't the right place for me from a long-term career standpoint. I was ready for more: more of a work challenge and certainly more income.

An Unwitting Dress Rehearsal

Fortunately, an old friend from my accounting days asked me to team up with him at his investment firm. He was a brilliant hedge fund manager, and he wanted me to head up the portfolio management part of the business. This was just what I was looking for, and I leaped at it. In this position, I took a leadership role in many of the client meetings and took yet another major step in improving my speech.

One of the biggest steps I took involved a mix of the two things that terrorized me my entire life: saying my name and talking on the phone. At my friend's investment firm, you were expected to say your name when you answered the phone—an unspoken requirement. Sure, other places I worked also had that expectation, but I always figured out a way around it by adding words before my name, like, "Hello, Larry Stein." But then I started to get stuck on the "Hello" part, which left me saying "Hell" without anything afterward—kind of embarrassing and terribly frustrating. That forced me to face this issue once and for all.

The other reason I had to address this issue was that concerns about answering the phone were taking up too much of my mental bandwidth. They were affecting my work. Every time a call came in, the ring startled me and panic set in, becoming more intense with each ring. It was the same thing every time: startle, panic, stutter. Boom, boom, boom. I was fifty-two years old, and I couldn't let it go on any longer; it was time to address this.

Fumbling for an answer, I experimented with each phase of the process—the ring, the reaction to the ring, the picking up of the phone, and then saying my name. The experiments led to the development of a chain reaction of behaviors that I would execute the exact same way every time, like a basketball player shooting a free throw. A process. I practiced that process so many times that it became automatic; I didn't have to think about it.

Here's the process: The phone rings, I smile, slowly pick up the phone, inhale a full breath, picturing my breath traveling up from my stomach and out my mouth, and speak on the exhale, the words riding on top of a waterfall of air: "Larry Stein." Just like that, the same way every time. Swish.

This was a major milestone in my life, much greater than I could perceive at the time. I was just trying to get through an embarrassing situation; I could not have imagined that every element of the process would become a foundational piece of my future improvement. I had no idea this would someday become a dress rehearsal for the signature event of my life, and the unwitting start to a new me—one who could face challenges and figure out new ways forward. Unfortunately, the job wasn't working out, and I had to make another change. This one would be for keeps; it almost had to be. I was fifty-four years old.

Happy Endings

Before we get to the next section of the book, there's something you should know: Most of the traumatic events from my childhood eventually had happy endings. It's amazing for me to look back and see how things turned out.

Remember all the fear I had as a child about reading from the Haggadah at my family's Passover seders? In my thirties, I was asked to lead a Passover seder for a handful of family members (by that time, most of the older generation had either passed away or was out of town). I agreed reluctantly (as always), but ended up loving it so much that I began leading Passover seders for my own family and friends. In fact, my own family seders became an annual tradition and one of my greatest joys. Sure, I stuttered a bit, but less and less as time went on. In my forties, I wrote and self-published my own Passover Haggadah, which sold thousands of copies nationwide. Decades after it was first published, I am still occasionally asked if I'm the Larry Stein who wrote *The Really Fun Family Haggadah*. Yes, I am.

Remember the experience of my bar mitzvah rehearsal? Well, I don't know what happened, but two days later, the actual event turned out to be a dream come true. I read and chanted flawlessly; I don't think I stuttered at all. I still can't believe it. Looking back, I often joke that my mom must have drugged me. That's the only conclusion that makes any sense. All I can remember is that she encouraged me to take a nap a few hours before the event. It's hard to imagine a thirteen-year-old boy would be calm enough to nap in such a situation, especially after experiencing such terror two days before. But sure enough, I went right to sleep. I woke up two hours later, got dressed, went to the synagogue with my family, and experienced the miracle of my life (to that point). It was truly a religious experience.

Years later as an adult, I became a more observant Jew and got the opportunity to occasionally lead Shabbat services in front of large synagogue congregations, chanting the type of passages I did on my bar mitzvah. I think my mom got to see me lead services once or twice, another miracle.

The Costs of Compromise

As for the fifth-grader who begged his mom to stay home from his school play, that story had a happy ending, too. In recent years, I have occasionally given speeches to business groups and even got paid for some of them, which is still hard for me to believe. I also gave a talk at the NSA Annual Convention (National Stuttering Association) and hope to give many more speeches for audiences who stutter. My mom always said, "Someday, you'll give speeches!" I laughed off that line time and again; it sounded too impossible. Now it doesn't, though I still find it hard to believe that anyone would pay me to speak.

Finally, what about the kid who was inspired by his dad's hobby to become an investment advisor but chose a different career because of his stuttering? Well, as you will read, I finally became an investment advisor and built the business of my dreams—small, but everything I always wanted. In the course of that dream, I wrote two investment books and have been interviewed numerous times by major media outlets for my views on the stock market and financial planning. Best of all, I have a client base of wonderful people who I treasure like family.

At the date of this writing, my mom and dad have been gone for decades, but their encouragement continues to push me forward. Two quotes come to mind in particular: Mom saying, "You can do anything you put your mind to" and Dad saying, "Just get out there and talk." I'm sure I was a source of great concern for them; I would like to think that somehow, they know things turned out okay for me, perhaps better than they could have possibly imagined.

Section 2:
Relearning to Speak

FOR SOMEONE WHO TRIES to plan everything, I'm amazed at how this journey took shape. Somehow, I was struck by an unlikely discovery, one thing led to another, and I kept going. I still can't believe it.

Pursuing the Dream

I was fifty-four years old, and it was time to do what I always wanted: to create my own investment firm. I thought I had finally made enough strides with my speech to build the business. I could now carry on long conversations, often without stuttering much. On the other hand, I still stuttered a lot when the pressure was on. I continued to fear difficult speaking situations and usually avoided them. Nonetheless, I thought I could make a go of the business.

My first year in business was magical. I built the firm according to my ethics and values in a field sadly lacking in both. It was a dream come true, a vision I had dating all the way back to the age of eleven. Moreover, in an incredible stroke of luck, email was becoming an accepted way of setting up business meetings, and I took full advantage of this revolution. It was too good to be true: I could set up meetings without making a phone call! I went crazy with this new power and set a goal of having at least ten network meetings per week, generally during breakfast and lunch. I even created my own network group, leading meetings of about fifteen small-business owners each month, all set up by email. My network grew and I gained some clients. At the end of the first year, I reflected with pride on all that I had accomplished.

There was just one problem: not enough clients. Not even close. Unfortunately, there's a big difference between casual conversations and the challenging discussions that lead to million-dollar accounts. I had become good at small talk, but businesses are built on big talk, the kind that closes major accounts. Fearing that I would stutter, I always avoided asking the tough questions that make new accounts possible, and my income reflected it. One of my sons had just graduated from an Ivy League school, and another was about to begin an even more expensive private school. I realized that if I didn't get more clients soon, I might have to look for a job.

And that would be a problem. Who would hire a fifty-five-year-old investment advisor with too few clients and a stuttering problem that kept him from calling new prospects, introducing himself, and asking the tough questions needed to close new accounts? Who would hire an investment advisor who couldn't even say his name? I knew exactly who: no one. How did I know? Because before I started my own firm, I tried calling friends in the business to see if they would hire me. The response was a gut punch: no. No one had an interest. None whatsoever. It was a shock. I was alone. After a lifetime of hoping someone would rescue me, I received the message loud and clear: Not this time. No one would rescue me. I would have to do this on my own.

The noose was starting to tighten; I had to act. Then it happened. Just when I wasn't thinking about it, in the most unlikely of moments, I realized something about my speech that changed my life forever.

An Unlikely Beginning

It was 9:45 at night, and I was walking out the door of the nonprofit after a board meeting. As I walked down the hallway to the front-door exit, I stopped near the door to get myself zipped up before walking out into the cold, snowy night, and suddenly, out of nowhere, it hit me: *I talk better when I public speak.*

What? Where did that come from? Stunned, I stopped dead in my tracks. I thought about it for a moment: When I lead board meetings, my speech is better than in regular conversations. And when I give presentations, my speech is better yet. In a matter of seconds, I made this life-changing decision: *Why don't I just public speak all the time! I'm going to throw away my old way of speaking and public speak all the time. From now on, I'm going to speak phrase to phrase. That's my mantra: phrase to phrase. Words and sounds no longer matter, only phrases.* Those were my exact words, all in a matter of twenty seconds. No thought, no planning. That was it: The moment that changed everything. I was propelled onto a new path; my life would never be the same.

When people ask me what was the "aha" moment that changed my speech, I say, "There really wasn't a single aha moment that changed it; there were a zillion aha moments strung together." But if I had to pick one moment among the many, this would be it. This was the turning point. I didn't realize it at the time, but this would be the first step of the greatest journey of my life. This was it: step one.

Sometimes a challenge is so massive, so daunting, that you have to give up to get where you want to go. You have to start over; there's no other way forward. That's how it was with my speech. I certainly wasn't getting anywhere with the way I was speaking. My speech was beyond fixing. It was the product of decades of poor speaking habits and destructive stuttering inclinations, far too much of a mess to expect success from applying a patch here or a bandage there. It was obvious to me: I had to give up my old way of speaking and start over, completely.

So, I started "public speaking" all the time. At this point, public speaking to me was simply a matter of talking in phrases with pauses in between, much as I had learned forty years ago at the University of Chicago. My new public speaking strategy seemed to have some merit. I could sense a bit of progress in my speech; it was palpable, an entirely new feeling. In a life filled with false starts and inevitable disappointment, this time seemed real.

The improvement was encouraging, but I was still a long way from being the effective communicator I needed to be to bring in clients and save my business. I had to do more. But what? I had failed at speech therapy so many times that it didn't seem like a viable option. Could I possibly improve my speech on my own?

My Life as a Mimic

Fortunately, I didn't have to improve my speech on my own. I had an expert instructor, Matt Lauer, the lead anchor of the *Today* show. Yeah, I know, years later he had his share of controversies, but he was about to change my life, though he didn't know it and probably never will. I was drawn to his speaking style: compelling, smooth, effortless, commanding. I was mesmerized; I could watch him all day.

I marveled at how clearly and effectively he communicated. As I watched him, I began to imagine that his words were coming out of my mouth. I even imagined the converse—that my words were coming out of his mouth. Soon, I was mimicking Matt Lauer, speaking and gesturing like him, the whole bit. Years later, I still find myself mimicking him. I could do Matt Lauer all day, and sometimes I still do.

The *Today* show became a daily master class for me, with Matt Lauer as my mentor. He taught me two of the main building blocks I would use to relearn to speak. Phrasing was the first. Of course, phrasing was nothing new to me, as mentioned earlier. But Matt Lauer turned phrasing into an art form. His phrasing was so clean and purposeful that it brought focus and clarity to his message. Inspired, I became a student of speaking mechanics. As I watched him, I kept wondering, *What is so compelling about his speech? Why do I always want to hear more?*

Soon it hit me: He was doing more than phrasing; he was drawing in his listeners by emphasizing words. By emphasizing a word in each phrase, he effectively underscored his key points. This was his way of telling you, "Hey, this is important, listen up!" I had been watching Matt Lauer for years, and until then, I had never noticed that he emphasized words. With this realization, emphasizing became the second pillar of my new speaking strategy. Now, in addition to phrasing, I would emphasize a word toward the end of every phrase.

Emphasizing words fostered further improvement in my speech. Encouraged, I began dissecting the speaking styles of TV personalities who I thought were particularly compelling. One of those speakers was Bob Woodward, of *Woodward and Bernstein* Watergate fame. He often appeared on panels of Sunday morning political shows. While other guests on these panels tended to race through their talking time to get in every point they could, Bob Woodward seemed to drone on, talking noticeably slower than the rest of the guests and accentuating his main points with strong emphasis and surprisingly long pauses between phrases.

The pauses distinguished him. They made him sound thoughtful, deliberate, and smart. I liked that; I wanted to sound like that. He was compelling, an inspiration to me as a person who stuttered. On a panel of fast talkers, he had the confidence to go slow. He commanded the stage simply by having the self-assurance to be authentic and different from everyone else. I mimicked Bob Woodward and built on my public speaking experiments with pausing to make it a foundational piece of my speaking mechanics. Years later, I heard the clever phrase "the power of the pause." I cannot agree more: Pausing is powerful. Pausing made my phrases distinct and gave me time to think and breathe; it became essential to my speaking process.

The more I watched broadcasters, the more I realized Matt Lauer wasn't the only one using emphasis. Nearly all broadcasters emphasized words; I just had never noticed it. They seemed to give each phrase a distinctive character, an intriguing drive. My fascination with the speaking of broadcasters continued, and even now, more than ten years later, I sometimes watch the news more interested in how it's being delivered than in the actual content. Soon I would learn that emphasizing words wasn't just an effective way to make a point; there was another benefit that perhaps even Matt Lauer didn't realize.

You Don't Breathe Right

Since I was susceptible to anxiety, stuttering was certainly not the only challenge I faced. Just as I was trying to work through my speech, a previous condition came back to haunt me: blepharospasm. This caused my eyes to blink involuntarily and incessantly, as if my blinking reflex were broken. It was brutal, torturous, and in some ways, even more exasperating than my stuttering.

On the other hand, at least there was a treatment, though I would try anything to avoid having to take it again: Botox. Injecting Botox deadened the nerves around my eyes and usually provided relief for a few months, maybe longer if I were lucky. But it's not a perfect solution. Even after the shots, I had to wait a few agonizing weeks before the Botox kicked in. My eyes drooped for weeks after the shots, and my right eye still slumps a bit to this day. The first set of shots I received were brutal, ten around each eye, without any painkiller. It was as if I were being attacked by an angry band of warriors shooting arrows into my eyes. I didn't want to go through that again if I didn't have to. (Later treatments with other doctors were far less traumatic.)

I mentioned my blinking issue to a friend, and she thought her yoga instructor might be able to teach me how to relax my eyes. Desperate for help, I eagerly made an appointment. The yoga instructor said to bring a check for a hundred dollars, which sounded reasonable. As the days ticked down before our appointment, I couldn't wait to meet him, hoping that he would be my ticket out of this insanity.

The day finally arrived. I climbed up the stairs to the yoga studio and found a large, long space decked out with tons of equipment but not a soul in sight. At first, I wasn't sure if I was in the right place; then the yoga instructor finally appeared. He was unlike anyone I had ever seen: impossibly broad shoulders with impossibly thin arms and waist, topped off with a shock of bright, bushy red hair reminiscent of Bozo the Clown. As we conversed, he watched me closely, eyeing me from head to toe.

After a few minutes, he moved in closer. He pressed his ear against my chest for an uncomfortably long time, maybe thirty seconds, maybe a few minutes. All I knew was that it was terribly awkward, almost to the point of feeling violated. Finally, he pulled away, paused, and offered his sage conclusion with a flick of his left hand. "You don't breathe right."

"Huh?" *Did he say breathe? What does that have to do with my eyes?*

"You don't breathe right. You take a breath and talk, but you never really clear out your breath. You take these little half-breaths. You need to clear out your air completely so you can take a fresh, full breath."

That was it? That was the sage advice of the great yoga instructor? I left the yoga studio stunned. That's all I got: "You don't breathe right?" Another hundred dollars down the drain. Story of my life: Putting my hopes in supposed experts, giving them money, and getting nothing for it. "You don't breathe right!" How was that going to help my eyes? Now what was I going to do? Give up and get those shots again?

As I walked back to my car down a long parking lot, those four words reverberated through my mind: "You don't breathe right." Ridiculous! The further I walked, the more they turned from ridiculous to something worth considering. *Wait, maybe he's right. Maybe I don't breathe right! Maybe that's impacting my speech?* Maybe the yoga instructor unwittingly gave me the solution I was seeking: Clear out my breath so I could take a fresh, full breath to start the next phrase.

Standing at my car door, I began to relate his comments to singing. I always breathe when I sing: big full breaths, and I never stutter. *Maybe there's something to it?* Singing was a personal refuge for me, the only way I could express myself vocally with total freedom. As I thought about it, the parallels between singing and speaking were stunning. Both use phrases. In singing, I begin with a breath, sing on the exhale, emphasize a word toward the end of the musical phrase, and start the next phrase with a fresh, full breath. Sure, there were differences between singing and speaking, but both seemed to share the basics of breathing, emphasizing, and phrasing. While phrasing and emphasizing were by now established parts of my speaking strategy, the concept of breathing began to captivate me—that would be my new focus. All that before I opened the car door.

THE AIRFLOW IMPERATIVE

As I thought more about the tie-in between singing and speaking, I did a bit of research. I learned that professional singers sing from their diaphragm, which science suggests is more effective than chest breathing. By singing from your diaphragm, you can draw a much greater breath and produce a more steady stream of air. According to breathing experts, chest breathing is best for running races; diaphragmatic breathing is ideal for speaking and singing.

I decided to make the switch to diaphragmatic breathing by lying down on my bed, holding my left hand on my stomach and my right hand on my chest. As I inhaled, I tried to have my stomach push my left hand up without elevating my right. Then, as I spoke, I tried to feel my stomach contract. It took a while, but eventually I made the switch. With a fuller breath and a stronger stream of air, I was able to speak a bit more effectively from phrase to phrase without gasping for air.

I became so impressed with the power of breathing that I decided to play a mind game to boost my improvement. I imagined that I would become more relaxed with every full breath I took. Just as I did when I was giving speeches for the nonprofit, I pictured my breath rising up from my diaphragm and out of my mouth, imagining that it flowed like a waterfall of air, with my words floating on top of the stream. I pictured my breath recirculating through me like a fountain, a fresh breath of air with every new phrase.

Airflow became a major focus of my speaking. To drive more airflow, I realized that I had to do more than just emphasize words; I had to become more expressive. I noticed that I often spoke in a flat, monotone voice, which restricted my airflow. Now being expressive became a focal point of my speaking—to be creative with my speech, making each phrase a bit different from the last. The more expressively I spoke, the stronger the airflow. Emphasizing words further strengthened my airflow. Matt Lauer emphasized words to make his speech more compelling; I used emphasis and expressiveness to drive airflow and clear out my breath to start the next phrase with a fresh, full breath.

I even began to picture my breathing as a sine wave, charting the flow of breaths in my mind. The breathing line rose as I inhaled to fill my lungs with air, then gradually declined as I spoke with expression.

With my remaining air, I emphasized a word toward the end of the phrase to clear out my breath and bring the line down to the bottom of the chart. Now I could take a fresh, full breath to start the cycle again. The key was to keep my air moving at all times, recirculating up and down in a nice, flowing sine wave. By contrast, the half-breaths of my prior speaking style left me with stagnant airflow and a relatively flat sine wave that made me more vulnerable to stuttering. The impact of this focus on airflow cannot be overstated; it was a game-changer for me.

Speaking became all about airflow. The words formed by the machinations of my mouth were now largely insignificant. Words were interchangeable, widgets of no distinction. Airflow was my engine. If my air was flowing, my speech would flow, too. I felt, *If I could breathe it, I could say it.* I relished the sense of airflow and rhythm, the feeling that I could say anything if the airflow was there. The feeling was soothing, calming, intoxicating—I couldn't get enough of it.

Years after I became comfortable with talking, I learned why breathing is so important to the speaking enterprise. Let's look at the science. Breathing brings oxygen to every cell of the body, especially the brain. If you're not getting enough oxygen to your brain, it may not function optimally (the dysfunction some call "brain fog"). This may make you more susceptible to stress, and you may not think as clearly as you would like. You may even have difficulty finding the right words to express yourself. That was me.

Given the science, it makes sense that I often felt like I was drowning when I got stuck in a hard block. I would gasp for air, sometimes even forgetting what I was going to say or what we were talking about. That changed for me when I became more expressive and used a lot of emphasis, enabling me to generate strong airflow and take fresh, full breaths to start each new phrase. Constant airflow and pausing between the phrases helped me to remain calm even in the heat of battle. It also gave me the time I needed to think on my feet, an entirely new capability that I found both surprising and empowering. As I would soon learn, there would be a lot more work to do on this front. Nonetheless, the mechanics of speaking were coming together for me.

The Strategy Is Set

Now, my strategy was set: Breathe, Emphasize, Phrase was born. I gave it a simple acronym, BEP, so I could easily remember the three steps and keep them top of mind. Take a breath, speak on the exhale with expression, emphasize a word late in the phrase to clear out my breath, then pause long enough to take a fresh, full breath to begin the next phrase. Easy—I could do this. I would now live phrase to phrase, breath to breath. BEP became my new way of speaking.

If you think about it, phrasing takes a massive problem—stuttering—that is so big and so complex that I don't understand it (I doubt that anyone truly does) and breaks it all down to one phrase at a time. Could I say full sentences without stuttering? Not consistently. But I could speak one phrase at a time, one after another. And that set me on an entirely new path, a feeling that I was on the verge of real progress.

I didn't invent BEP; it's just the basics of how good speakers speak. Of course, TV broadcasters do more with their speech than BEP, but I needed to keep it simple for myself: consistent execution was more important than perfect speaking. BEP made sense to me. It also made me sound natural. There was no need to hide with BEP, unlike other techniques that made me sound robotic. I was now speaking better than ever, though I was still stuttering heavily in the heat of battle.

To those who don't stutter, the phrase "speaking in the heat of battle" may sound like a childish exaggeration. But to those of us who stutter, it's entirely appropriate. Some speaking situations can make us feel like we're actually in the heat of battle. The glare of spotlights when asked a question, the panic of time pressure, the bewilderment of a block: These are all heat-of-the-battle moments, and for me, they occurred many times a day, just about every day of my life. My speech was improving with BEP, but in the heat of battle, the strategy went out the window and not by choice; it's just that the situation at hand would overwhelm me.

Boxer Mike Tyson had a great line: "Everyone has a plan until they get punched in the face." Stuttering was my punch in the face. Once I started stuttering on a word, it led to more stutters, and pretty soon, I was struggling on nearly every word. It was as if I got caught up in a hurricane of stuttering and swept up in the swirl, totally overwhelmed.

I wondered, *Why does that happen to me but not to the other 330 million Americans who speak so effortlessly, even in the heat of battle? They seem to have an idea, and—poof—it comes out of their mouths. There's no thinking. It's easy. It's easier than easy; it just happens. As effortless as breathing. They don't even think about it.*

By contrast, all I did was think about my speech. The more I thought, the worse it got. That's it, I decided: No more thinking. I had a strategy that made sense—BEP—but I had to be able to execute it without thinking about it. It had to be easy; it had to flow out of my mouth as naturally as breathing. It had to be automatic.

Make It Automatic

I thought about things I did that were automatic. When I played tennis with friends years ago, I didn't plan every step of my stroke—if I did, I would never get off a shot—it was automatic, so I didn't have to think about it. It's the same with driving a car or riding a bike; they're automatic. Having played high school sports, I knew what it took to make things automatic: sheer repetition. But that was never my strong suit. I was never big on practice and working out—that would have to change.

It has become popular to say that it takes ten thousand hours to master something, a number quoted by Malcolm Gladwell in his book *Outliers: The Story of Success*. I didn't know about Gladwell's book when I started my journey, but I knew one thing for sure: Turning around fifty years of stuttering wasn't going to happen overnight. Nor was it going to happen because of positive thinking or clever insights.

There was no way around it: I would have to put in the reps—a lot of them. I couldn't do too many. Just as a casual runner wouldn't think of running a marathon without extensive training, I was now in training. I had to practice speaking with BEP so much and get in so many reps, that I built muscle memory as well as mental memory. BEP had to be automatic, it had to be as natural as breathing.

My BEP practice was to read a paragraph or two, then summarize what I had just read. That's what I did over and over: read, then summarize. The goal was to get my talking BEP to be as good as my reading BEP. I can't remember how many minutes a day I practiced or how many times a day—it didn't matter. Weeks of intense practice paid off. Eventually, BEP kicked in and became the only way in which

I would read or summarize. I learned something in these weeks of intense practice that would become my carrying card going forward: Hard work wins.

BEP was now automatic, at least in the privacy of my room. No thinking, no effort—it just rolled off my tongue as natural as breathing. I didn't even have to plan my phrases; the words just seemed to fall in line. Each phrase started with a fresh, full breath and concluded with an emphasized word. Breathe, Emphasize, Phrase was now easy and natural; it was me. It was time for the next step: to bring BEP into the big, bad world. But how would I take that leap? What would be my process? I soon learned that I wouldn't have to take a leap at all.

If You Can't Go Big, Go Small

Bold leaps are heroic, celebrated. The bigger, the better. Motivational speakers shout, "Go for it!" They pound the table and say, "Go big or go home!" We're inundated with stories about bold, brash business leaders who set big, hairy, audacious goals and plow through them with admirable grit and moxie. That's great in business and sports; go after all the big, hairy, audacious goals you want.

But it's not for people who stutter. At least, not for me. Maybe I was too damaged. Or maybe stuttering is just a different animal. Believe me, I've spent a lifetime trying to take big, bold leaps, and I've always ended up in the same place—splat, face down on the floor, falling back to square one.

In my younger days, I was often fooled by illusions of confidence. I would have a good conversation, maybe even a good day or week of talking; it was exciting, encouraging. Like seeing an oasis in the desert, I hung on for dear life to any shred of confidence I could. My hopes would rise, thinking maybe this was my moment, that maybe I was finally done with stuttering. Then it would happen: A bad block would lead to a bad conversation, a bad day of speaking, a bad week, and soon those shreds of confidence slipped through my fingers. Poof, gone, like they were never there.

I was sick of square one. I had to do something different, and this was it: If you can't go big, go small. I decided to go really small. Baby-steps small. One small step at a time. It would be a much longer process, maybe even laborious, but that was okay with me as long as I could finally improve my speech. Instead of seeking a quick fix as I always had, I prepared myself for the long haul. I was committed to go the distance and do the work, however long it took. I decided this time would be different. It had to be; my future depended on it. I had to build my business, or it could become an ugly situation for both me and my family.

Small steps made sense to me. I had always broken down big problems into smaller ones, whether it was with math, sports, or other challenges; it was my established mode of problem-solving. Maybe I could take the massive monolith of stuttering, break it into small steps, and finally make some progress. I was resolved to go all out.

No Step Is Insignificant

I had already taken the first two steps: To read and summarize to myself with BEP, then make it automatic. Now, I had to take the next step: To take BEP from my bedroom into the outside world. This next step seemed daunting, like a leap across a canyon. I had to make it seem small, smaller than small, almost insignificant.

To make it as insignificant as possible, I realized the next step was clear: To speak with my wife using BEP. I hardly ever stuttered with Susan, and that's what made it the perfect next step. She was always the one I could talk with, the one who put me at ease. There would be no question of fluency; it would simply be an opportunity to build a skill. She would be the perfect bridge step from speaking in private to bringing BEP into the real world. There would be no leap, just the next step in a natural progression.

Using BEP with Susan went smoothly. I don't think she noticed anything different in the course of normal conversation between us, which made the transition even easier. So far, so good. Small step, small success. Score it.

The next small step was also obvious: Using BEP with my kids over the phone. This would be another small step that bordered on being insignificant. I almost never stuttered with them. It would have been an easier small step if they still lived at home, but by this time, they were adults living far away, so the phone would have to do. But that actually worked out even better since it also gave me practice using BEP on the phone—I got a two-fer with this one. Another small step, another small success. It felt good. I learned there are no insignificant steps as long as you take another step closer toward your goal.

I started with easy interactions—my wife and my kids—so far, so good. The next small step, speaking with friends, wouldn't be so insignificant. In the past, I tended to limit my conversations with friends to short quips, just brief enough to give me an opportunity to speak without much stuttering. Sure, I was an active participant in most conversations, but I always played it safe, trying to stay within the bounds of speaking without stuttering: keep it short, keep it fun, stick with pet phrases. Now, I would move on to new ground, speaking in more complete sentences, maybe even going so far as to tell stories. Boundaries would be broken.

Emerging Shoots of Confidence

I still remember that first story. I felt like a baby deer gathering my legs underneath me, gaining the confidence to take that first step. It may sound like an overstatement, but at that time, so early in my journey, telling a story to a bunch of friends was life-changing. I started slowly, feeling my way through the phrases, gathering confidence. Soon, I felt the power to express myself in full. It was my first glimpse at how it might feel to speak freely, to say everything I wanted to say, to hold nothing back. I can still remember the surge of hope coursing through me as I envisioned a future I could never previously imagine. Now I could: becoming free to speak seemed like a real possibility.

Relearning to Speak

I loved my newfound capability. No longer was I sitting in the corner, saying the bare minimum, a cute quip here or there, or nothing at all. Now, I was a raconteur holding court. And I loved the court. No longer did I wilt under the glare of a thousand spotlights; I welcomed it. The more eyes on me, the better. I basked in their responses: a smile here, a laugh there. Sure, I was still stuttering now and then, but I finally felt that I could express myself without holding back. The freedom was empowering. I was like a little kid with a shiny new toy. I had so much to say. One story led to another, and soon I couldn't stop. The ball kept rolling. For the first time in my life, I felt that I was on my way.

In my younger days, I was often fooled by false starts and illusions of confidence. Taking small steps changed all that. Rather than rely on hope, I put in the work, one small step at a time. With each small step, each small success, my confidence grew. Sure, I was tempted to speed up the process, abandon the small-step strategy, and take a leap out of my comfort zone. But after failing to improve my speech for decades, I knew I was vulnerable to disappointment. Failing and suffering a bad setback might shatter my fragile confidence, maybe even lead me to give up entirely. I couldn't let that happen again; it wasn't worth the risk. I was determined to remain patient and disciplined, trust the process, and stick with small steps.

A Hierarchy of Small Steps

My first few steps were encouraging. Gaining confidence in my speech was a completely new feeling for me; I wanted more. These early successes led me to construct a hierarchy, like rungs on a ladder, of how I could progress toward my goals. I can't remember the actual steps, and I'm sure my path wasn't as linear as it could have been. After all, I was learning on the fly, taking stabs at one experiment after another. It wasn't the most efficient process, but I was finally making progress and that was good enough for me. Here's the broad outline of my hierarchy:

1. Learn BEP in private. Practice reading a paragraph or two of an article, then summarize it.

2. Practice BEP so much that it becomes automatic.

3. Try BEP with my easiest audiences: first my wife and kids, then friends, acquaintances, and easy business situations.

4. Build up to work situations of increasing difficulty.

5. Introduce myself in low-pressure phone calls to businesses, like hotels and hardware stores.

6. Work up to saying my name and introducing myself in real situations.

Again, this was just a broad outline of how I took BEP out of the bedroom and into the real world. There were so many more steps involved, many of which arose unexpectedly in my climb up the ladder. Some steps were so daunting, such as saying my name, that I developed entire hierarchies just to achieve them. Although new challenges seemed to arise from time to time, the basic process was always the same: start with the easiest step, advance to the next easiest step, and keep progressing up the ladder one small step at a time.

As I progressed up my hierarchy and became emboldened by small successes, I realized that I was in the midst of an adventure. It was exciting. New challenges were always popping up, making my hierarchy a dynamic, living concept. I was constantly finding new steps to squeeze into the ladder. The process never seemed to end. In retrospect, that was good. It showed that I was seeking new opportunities for growth.

It's interesting to note that several years after I improved my speech, I learned that my hierarchy of small steps was nothing new—it's actually well-established science. Psychologists call it "exposure therapy." A psychologist constructs a hierarchy of a patient's fears ranked according to difficulty, then begins by exposing the patient to easy situations and progressing up to more difficult ones.

I had no idea what I was doing, but I liked where I was going. I seemed to be developing traction, the ability to move forward with only brief setbacks, like a cogwheel train climbing a mountain. This wasn't one of those momentary feel-good illusions that always ended in disappointment. No, this time was different. The climb was slow, but for once in my life, it felt sure.

FREE TO SPEAK

COMPARTMENTALIZING BAD PLAYS

Making BEP automatic was paying dividends. In the past, stuttering came in clumps. Once I suffered a heavy block, more were sure to follow until my speech completely fell off the rails. It was as if I were stuck in an electrical circuit, one block generating more blocks in a continuous loop, sometimes leading to days or weeks of difficult stuttering. During those times, when I wanted to speak, the pressure would be so palpable that I could feel it pressing against my face, so overwhelming that I expected to stutter every time I spoke for days or weeks on end. With BEP, the clumps of stuttering were less severe, less frequent, and didn't last as long, but they still arose from time to time.

In trying to solve this problem, I hearkened back to sports. Isn't it amazing how a top-flight pro football quarterback can throw a seemingly disastrous interception and come back in the next series to lead his team to victory? How do they do that? And how could I bring that mentality to my speech? From what I've read, top quarterbacks compartmentalize bad plays. They don't let one bad play affect their next. They put the bad play aside and move on to achieve their next objective as if nothing bad ever happened.

Why couldn't I do that with my speech? Why did one hard block have to lead to days or weeks of heavy stuttering? How could I compartmentalize my speech? And then I thought, *Doesn't phrasing naturally compartmentalize my speech?* Each phrase is its own compartment. Just as quarterbacks live one play at a time, I adopted the mindset that I would "live one phrase at a time." It fit neatly with my "living phrase to phrase" approach. If I stuttered badly on one phrase, no big deal, there would be a zillion phrases right after it. Rather than stew about it, I would laugh it off. I wasn't going to let an interception or a bad block get to me anymore. I would simply move on to the next phrase. In football, they call it "having a short memory."

But what if I were stuck in the circuit effect? How could I get back on track before things got completely out of control? What was my way out? I had to break the circuit. Stop mid-block, go back to the beginning of the phrase, and execute the cleanest BEP I could muster. I called it "the integrity of a phrase" since the goal was to say a phrase with such clean BEP (integrity) that I felt I could say anything. I would overdo every aspect of BEP: take overly full breaths, over-emphasize words, be overly expressive, shorten my phrases so I breathe more often and generate stronger airflow, play with the pauses in between phrases—do anything to break the circuit. Today, I call it "BEP Extreme." The key to breaking the circuit is doing something totally different than what you were doing before. That's why overdoing each aspect of BEP is so effective. It breaks you out of your previous stuttering paradigm. Pull every lever of BEP you can to break the circuit and get back on track.

It felt so good to break the circuit and get back on track that I came up with a celebration I called "winning the phrase." I would literally say to myself, "I won the phrase." Years later, I learned there is substantial research about celebrating successes. A tenet of Cognitive Behavioral Therapy, celebrating successes can help cement new behaviors and lead to additional positive outcomes. A 2011 *Harvard Business Review* article entitled "Small Wins and Feeling Good" by Teresa Amabile and Steve Kramer notes that small wins can help lift people out of depression. Stanford researcher BJ Fogg, in his book *Tiny Habits*, talks about how celebrating tiny victories can accelerate the pace of learning new habits. It was encouraging to break the circuit and get back on track, but why was speaking still so hard in difficult speaking situations? What was holding me back?

Section 3:
Retraining My Brain

I THOUGHT THAT IMPROVING my speech mechanics with BEP would be enough to get me where I wanted to go: to speak well enough to build my business. I was wrong; not even close. BEP provided the essential foundation needed to make progress with my speech, but I still had a long way to go, much longer than I expected.

Starting at Zero

In 1961, John F. Kennedy said, "
We will land a man on the moon."

In 1987, Ronald Reagan said,
"Mr. Gorbachev, tear down this wall."

And in 2011, I said, … "Zero."

That's right: Zero. Zero was huge. Momentous. Life-changing. When you can't go big, go small. I started smaller than small; I started at zero.

There was nothing special about this moment. No lead up, no anticipation. It was just another business conversation, and I was about to do a typical word substitution: I would always stutter on "zero," so I would say "O" instead. I'm in the investment business, so I substituted zero all the time. No biggie. It was standard procedure for me; I did word substitutions all day, every day of my life.

Somehow, this time was different. The cycle started as usual. I felt myself shrink from the challenge of saying the word I intended and prepared my usual substitution. Then it happened. For reasons I still don't understand, I chose this one, magical moment to stand up to the challenge and say something so simple yet so life-changing. I said, "zero."

That was it: I faced it and beat it. On that fateful day in 2011, that endless loop of mind-numbing calculations met its first speed bump. It was only a single momentary stop in the crazed frenzy that was my mind, but it was a start. For once, I didn't give in and fall down the word-substitution rabbit hole. At least not this time.

Fifty Years of Stuttering Really Messed Me Up

Saying zero was the start of something new. The climb up my hierarchy was bringing me into new speaking situations and presenting challenges that pushed me to the point of becoming more aware of my stuttering inclinations, such as avoiding speaking, anticipating stuttering, and word substitution. At this point, these stuttering inclinations were a bit disturbing but easily dismissible as part of my everyday stuttering life. No big deal, I figured; it's just part of being a person who stutters.

Then it happened. One day, in the course of taking a new small step up my hierarchy, I realized something that stunned me, like a shovel hitting me over the top of my head: fifty years of stuttering really messed me up. Suddenly, my stuttering inclinations were being exposed as if they were lit up by the glaring lights of a prison watchtower, too bright to ignore, even for me. I couldn't dismiss them as benign any longer. It became clear: my stuttering inclinations were sabotaging me.

Too much of my mental bandwidth was being used for destructive purposes. My mind raced incessantly, it never shut off. I was a slave to my stuttering inclinations. I could barely think of anything else. If I was ever going to significantly improve my speech and reach my goals, I had to do something about this.

But how? Improving my speaking mechanics required sheer effort and reps, I could do that; but delving into my mind was another matter. My knowledge of psychology amounted to nothing more than Psych 100 in the first semester of college. A lot of good that would do me. I never had to study: my fraternity had the answers to all the tests!

Nonetheless, I had to do something. I had to turn back the clock on fifty years of stuttering, reversing the labyrinth of stuttering inclinations that silently manipulated my life. I felt like a prisoner trapped inside a hardened shell. It was as if I added one stuttering inclination after another over the decades, like slapping strips of paper-mâché on a ball. The strips pile up, harden, and eventually form a shell. Now imagine how deep and dense that shell had become after fifty years of stuttering. I had to break that shell.

I had to face my stuttering inclinations in a showdown that ultimately came down to a binary choice: break it or reinforce it. For decades, I took the easy way out and stuck with the status quo, reinforcing my stuttering inclinations, making them stronger and giving them the fuel they needed to keep me in their grip. It was as if I were feeding a beast that craved more and more meat.

It became clear to me that breaking these inclinations would require an intense effort unlike any I had ever attempted. I couldn't just tinker around the edges as usual; this time had to be different. Whatever I did had to be more explosive, more radical. I had to shock my stuttering and my stuttering inclinations. I had to do the opposite.

Think Opposite, Do Opposite

Here's what I did: Every time I noticed a stuttering inclination, I stopped myself and did a quick, real-time evaluation: Is it destructive and holding me back? If so, I would ask the next-level question: What would be the exact opposite? Whatever the opposite would be, I did it. I even developed a hand motion to cue myself, flipping my hands over each other as if to say, "Do the opposite!" I would literally stop myself in the middle of conversations, think for a moment, do my hand motion, and do the opposite. I don't think anyone noticed what I was doing, but my brain certainly did. Doing the opposite gradually began to have a significant impact on my speech and how I lived.

No inclination was safe, I attacked as many as I could. For example, rather than move away from a potential conversation, I moved toward it. Instead of struggling through a block, I would stop, surrender, smile, go back to the beginning of a phrase, and start over with a fresh, full breath and the cleanest BEP I could muster. Rather than answer a question with the fewest words possible to avoid stuttering, I did the opposite, lengthening my responses to tell the whole story and sometimes even more. Instead of avoiding people and viewing them with contempt (how's that for a rationalization to avoid people!), I made it a personal mission to smile and engage with every person in the friendliest way possible. Everything the opposite.

One thought at a time, one habit at a time, I retrained my brain by doing the opposite over and over. I pictured my stuttering as a massive monolith, like the one in the movie *2001: A Space Odyssey*. Every time I did the opposite, I chipped away at one of the many inclinations supporting the monolith. Eventually, I chipped away at my inclinations so much that, one by one, they gave way and imploded, weakening the hold stuttering had on me. Think opposite, do opposite became an obsession. I found the process to be endlessly fascinating. It was as if I were doing science experiments on my mind.

The world became my laboratory, and in a sense, I became a laboratory. The laboratory of me was intriguing, often leading to new realizations about my speech and myself. One of my most important laboratory findings was that I had to break myself to be myself. Doing the opposite was my tool of choice. If I avoided speaking situations, I would break it and engage. If I was hurrying my sentences, I would break it and speak slowly in short phrases with longer pauses between the phrases. Break, break, break. The more I broke things in my speech and in my brain, the better I spoke and the more relaxed I became—and the more I became my true self.

Years later, I learned there is actual science behind doing the opposite. Cognitive Behavioral Therapy (CBT) posits that bad experiences can be marked so strongly in our brains, specifically the amygdala, that whenever a similar situation occurs again, the bad memory is triggered. For me, that bad memory was stuttering and everything tied to it: the emotions and the physical responses. CBT suggests that those memories can be changed if, immediately after the bad experience occurs, the person has a success that is the opposite of the previous failure. Self-talk is a part of this process. The strategy is to challenge the negative self-talk, evaluate your thoughts one at a time, and do the opposite of those false beliefs.

And that's what I was doing. By doing the opposite and chipping away at that massive monolith, my stuttering inclinations began to give way. My speech improved, and I improved as a person. I avoided less and became more responsible and more mature. Babied all my life because of my stuttering, I was finally starting to grow up. In my desperation to effect personal change, I lucked into doing the opposite, and it changed my life.

Playing with My Speech

I was always on the lookout for ways in which my stuttering inclinations were sabotaging me. Some of these moments were nuanced and difficult to detect. Others were patently blatant, almost to the point of being ridiculous. Here's one.

I was invited by a networking acquaintance to take part in a one-day class he was teaching on public speaking. Considering the public speaking I did with the nonprofit, I felt pretty comfortable taking the offer. Once I arrived, I learned why the instructor offered the class to me for free: He had only two other people in the room; I was the third. This would be good practice for me, I figured, since it was about as low-pressure as you can get, especially considering I would probably never see these people again.

Yet, there I was, standing in front of the group to give my first three-minute presentation, holding on for dear life, trying not to stutter. It seemed to go pretty well: a few hesitations, some moments of uncertainty, and some minor blips but no real stuttering. *Phew, I got past that one.* I was feeling good about it until the instructor called out from the back of the room, "Hey, that was good. But why don't you smile?"

"I smiled," I replied.

"Not during the presentation."

I became defensive. "Well, I'm talking about my business, I take it seriously."

"So serious that you can't smile?"

An hour later, it was my turn for my next three-minute presentation. Before I began, he called out, "Now smile, all right?"

I nodded as I walked up to my spot in front of the group. Just to humor him, I tried to smile during the presentation. But I couldn't. As much as I tried, I just couldn't smile. Nor could I smile during the third and final three-minute talk. That's how rigid I was; I couldn't even smile! If I was that tight for a three-minute presentation in front of three people I would never see again, think of how rigid I was in speaking situations of consequence. I knew what I had to do. I had to do the opposite: I had to play with my speech.

I hearkened back to my teens when I sold clothes at my dad's store: It was the first time I came up with the crazy idea of playing with my speech. His store was forty miles away from our home, and oddly enough, I found that liberating. No one knew me; more importantly, no one knew I stuttered. I could experiment with my identity and, in turn, my speech. Working at my dad's store became the early foundational experience for one of the most important experiments I would ever attempt with my speech.

Now, more than thirty-five years later, I would try to play with my speech again. Frankly, it didn't come easy; it was such a radical change from my rigid way of speaking. Why so rigid? I didn't know at first, but one day I realized that I was literally fighting to be fluent.

Even if I wasn't stuttering, my speech was still halting and hesitant, all to avoid stuttering. It became clear to me: I had to give up the fight. It was a battle I couldn't win. So I surrendered and did the opposite: I played with my speech. I became more expressive and tried to have fun talking. Giving up the fight led me to an entirely new paradigm of speaking: a paradigm of play.

Playing with my speech did not come naturally to me. Awkward at first, the adjustment came slow and rocky, and I felt out of my element. It took a while, but eventually, I found the fun in speaking. Breathe, Emphasize, Phrase became a free-flowing expression of the message I was trying to convey and the audience I was trying to reach. Speaking became fun, liberating, even relaxing.

Being more expressive with my speech led to being more expressive with my hands. Without even thinking about it, I naturally began gesturing in tandem with emphasizing words. I found that the more emphatically I gestured, the more expressive I became and the more freely my air flowed. Airflow became my engine and expressiveness my paintbrush, replacing the rigidity that kept me so stiff. Speaking was now an art form.

I didn't realize it at the time, but years later, I can see that playing with my speech led me to adopt some of the mannerisms of the comedian Jerry Seinfeld: the pause to impress a point, the changes in speed and tone, the shift to short phrases when nearing a punchline, smiling while talking, and so on. These were all experiments for me, radical changes, 180s. I found the process exhilarating, as if I were creating a new me.

Taking the Offensive

Radical change led me to discover an entirely different mindset. Rather than be rigid and defensive and wait for a stutter to happen, I took the offensive. Now, I dictated the action, pulling the various levers of Breathe, Emphasize, Phrase like I was conducting a symphony, calling on the full range of instruments at my disposal to deliver the optimal sound. I breathed when I wanted to start a new phrase, not when I had to because I anticipated a stutter. I made phrasing a creative pursuit, playing with the length of phrases and the pauses in between. Rather than let stuttering control my speech, I took control.

Taking the offensive became a mindset that transcended speaking; it became the mode of operation for my life. Rather than be defensive and watch life pass me by, I began to take responsibility for my actions. Rather than avoid situations and turn down opportunities, I opened myself up to new possibilities and sought out new situations. No longer was I going to let stuttering hold me back.

After decades of saying "no" to life, I was now saying "yes": yes to taking responsibility for my speech and yes to taking on new speaking opportunities. I even took on new responsibilities in my life. Building my business was just one of many; I was also becoming more responsible with respect to our home life. I could feel myself growing, working through challenges, and dealing with the responsibilities of being an adult.

The shift from being defensive to taking the offensive impacted so many aspects of my life. It was perhaps the ultimate opposite. Stuttering is defensive by nature: rigid, reactive, fearful, and avoiding. Taking the offensive is the exact opposite: playful, proactive, confident, and engaging. There was no hiding. See a challenge, take it, bring it on. The more I took the offensive, the more I took on those qualities. I was changing, maturing. Emboldened, I felt I was ready to take on the big kahuna of stuttering challenges: the anticipation cycle.

Breaking the Anticipation Cycle

The anticipation cycle was probably born out of self-preservation, a desperate attempt to get out a sentence without stuttering. It used to make perfect sense: Keep on the lookout for words that might make me stutter and avoid them by substituting a word I thought I could say. And while I searched for a new word, throw in filler words like umms and uhhs to keep the sound going until I thought I could speak without stuttering. Perfect sense.

Until now. No longer did I need to substitute words or toss in filler words like umms and uhhs. Now I had a speaking strategy (BEP) and a process for improvement (small steps) that I believed in, and with good reason: I was getting results. One success after another, I was gaining trust in BEP. I felt that if I could breathe it, I could say it. Rather than avoid words and insert substitute and filler words, I could do the opposite and say what I wanted. Exactly what I wanted. Maybe now I could finally break this insanity.

Saying "zero" rather than "O" was the unwitting start of this effort. The new goal was to speak that way all the time: no substitutions, no fillers. And if I stuttered, I stuttered; let the chips fall where they may. I could accept that. Substituting words reinforced the fear of saying certain words and kept my brain chugging in overdrive, while filler words messed up my breathing by using up the air that should be expended to say the actual words I wanted to say. Whatever utility filler words may have had in the past, illusory at that, they had no value now. They had to go.

Phrase by phrase, I summoned the courage to speak without crutches, the discipline to stick with my original words and eschew editing: to say exactly what I wanted to say. Proving that I could say what I wanted time after time, I realized that the urge to substitute words and insert fillers was melting away. And though I may have stuttered more in the early going, breaking the anticipation cycle proved to be one of the most important improvements to my speech and my life.

Once I was no longer caught up in the endless calculation of word substitutions and filler words, something absolutely amazing happened: My mind slowed to a comfortable hum. I began to sense a calm I could never have imagined, much deeper than any relaxation technique or therapy I had tried. At the same time, I seemed to become much more resourceful. I could never have anticipated the enormous impact of stopping the anticipation cycle and freeing my mental bandwidth.

Previously, it was as if nearly all of my mental bandwidth was gobbled up by the insanity of anticipating stuttering. Now, with so much more of my brain available, my mind is much clearer and ideas seem to flow more easily from mind to mouth. I can think on my feet and be resourceful—that was never me. While I can certainly see and feel the effects of aging, in some ways, I find that I can now think more effectively than ever. Cleared from the clutter, I am still exploring the extent of my capabilities.

Enjoy Every Conversation

An undeniable momentum was building, pushing me to search for more inclinations to flip on their heads. It was as if I were trudging through a jungle, machete in hand, slashing my way through the dense foliage on the hunt for my next prey. And then, I found something lurking in the brush that had been staring at me my entire life: the act of speaking itself.

At about this time, I became friendly with a guy who smiled as he talked—not just once in a while, but all the time. He was the nicest guy in the world, and it showed, right there on his face. I was amazed at how effortlessly he talked, smiling all the way.

Admiring how easily he spoke, I decided to add this element to my repertoire: I would smile as I talked. After all, smiling is the opposite of the rigidity in stuttering, maybe it would have a positive impact. And it did: the impact was immediate and significant. I found that I stuttered less and enjoyed talking more. Maybe the public speaking instructor had a point after all.

Smiling led me to an even more important initiative: to enjoy every conversation. Enjoying speaking was almost the perfect opposite of stuttering, a powerful agent for change. Whether in person or on the phone, I committed myself to enjoying every time I talked. No exceptions, no matter what the situation. You might wonder: "How can you enjoy difficult conversations?" Let's go through some examples. Grilled about a work matter, I could enjoy sharing my knowledge and defusing a situation. Hearing bad news, even about a person passing away, I could still, in a sense, "enjoy" comforting a friend or loved one as best I could. Sure, it was a different type of enjoyment, sometimes even filled with tears, but I could still "enjoy" doing my best for the other person. If you look through rose-colored glasses, every conversation, even painful ones, can be "enjoyed."

What did this do? Enjoying conversations had a positive impact on my speech and on my relationships with others. I was connecting more deeply; my interactions were taking on a richer texture. As much of a change as this was for me, my next experiment may have had an even greater impact.

GIVE, GIVE, GIVE

In the past, I was so focused on trying to get around my stuttering that I didn't realize the effect it was having on me, not just on my speech but on me as a person. More than once in the past, my wife commented, "You're so focused on what you want to say that you don't hear what others are talking about." I dismissed her comment for years, saying to myself, *No, that can't be me. I'm a devoted father and husband! I'm not self-absorbed! I give of myself to my wife and kids all the time!*

Years later, as I worked through my speech and progressed up my hierarchy, I began to have some doubts about that answer. Maybe she had a point? Maybe I *was* too self-absorbed? Maybe I was so caught up with my stuttering that I didn't think of others or what they had to say? But, hey, I had a good reason for that: Until my recent improvement, I had been in survival mode all the time, just trying to make it through the day. Can't you see that?

Okay, it seemed logical, but was it valid? Was survival mode the best I could do, even when I was stuttering heavily? And wasn't survival mode harmful to my speech, turning me too inward and keeping the focus on my stuttering? Could this have made it more difficult for me to break out of my stuttering shell and improve my speech? After all, when you walk down a steep flight of stairs and focus on the steps too intently, you're more likely to trip. Ugh, that was me: I was tripping over my stuttering all the time! I had to change this.

Once again, I thought about the opposite. This one was easier: The opposite of being self-absorbed was to give. So I decided that rather than focus on myself, I would give to others. I would make giving my mode of operation in everything I did. Regardless of the type of interaction, I shifted my focus to other people. I focused on being a giver. At first, I was a bit clumsy with my giving, but soon I got the hang of it. Giving became one of my greatest joys. I even coined a phrase with my kids, encouraging them to "give, give, give."

The impact of becoming a giver was entirely unexpected. I thought this would be a minor tweak in the way I lived my life. It wasn't; it was life-changing. By giving, I started to truly listen to others, ask questions, and appreciate them for who they really were. Sure, I had already begun to enjoy conversations, but this was a higher, more authentic level of enjoyment. As I thought about my relationships, I realized how little I really knew about people I thought I knew well. That would change. The paradigm shift to giving made me a better conversationalist, a better friend, and frankly, a better person. I actually cared about something and someone beyond myself. It felt good. It felt right.

Giving also made a huge impact on my speech. Rather than feel the glare of a thousand spotlights every time I talked, I placed the focus on others, trying to give them what they needed. Instead of feeling that every speaking situation was a high-wire test to avoid stuttering or was a referendum on me, I began to view conversations as an opportunity to learn about others and build relationships that mattered. I started to feel a new sense of calm as I spoke. I made peace with speaking, and I made peace with others. We were friends now, no longer competitors. The battle was over; I just wanted to give.

Years later I would learn there is scientific evidence that shows the positive impact of giving. Studies suggest that people who give their time to their community or to charitable organizations have higher self-esteem, less depression, and lower stress levels than those who are not involved. The more I gave, the more I felt those traits take hold.

Frankly, I don't know if I could have made such an improvement in my speech if I didn't become a giver. I was too self-absorbed. When I stuttered a lot, I would turn inward, get down and roll around in the muck of it all, and reinforce my negative thoughts. Stuttering became a self-fulfilling prophecy, and I didn't have a way out because I was so focused inwardly. Giving changed that. Rather than turn inward, I turned outward, looking to give in whatever way I could. My worldview shifted; my personal paradigm changed.

My Two Goals for Every Conversation

Now, in every conversation, I have two goals: to give and to enjoy. First, I want to give the other person something of myself, whether it's knowledge, respect, empathy, or just a smile. Whatever I believe that person needs, I try to give. Sometimes, it's asking questions to learn more about them, and other times, it's taking a back seat in the conversation to let them fully express themselves. Every situation is different. Sometimes, the best way to give is to simply be silent and listen intently. Either way, my focus is on them, not on me and my speech.

Second, as I mentioned previously, I want to enjoy every conversation, even if it's a difficult situation. Sometimes, the enjoyment is in learning about the person, their past, and their perspectives. Other times, it may just be sharing a laugh or a smile. In all cases, it's finding the joy in human give and take, and connecting with each other.

Think about the massive shift this had on me: By giving and enjoying every conversation, I took the pressure off my stuttering and placed my focus on the other person. I changed the metric of success in my interactions from how much I stuttered to how much I enjoyed the moment. Isn't this how the rest of the world views their conversations? Giving was personally rewarding and became a profound source of enjoyment; the two became intertwined. Conversations became so much more meaningful to me because I was engaged with the other person instead of with my speech. This paradigm shift had a sea-change impact on my speech and my life. The pressure was off, the enjoyment was on.

Tapping My Inner Toolkit

Even with my growing confidence, climbing my hierarchy to the highest rungs sometimes led to challenges that stymied me, leaving me to wonder how I could possibly achieve the next goal. Had I bumped up against my ceiling? Was this as far as I could go? Those questions spurred me on to discover something new inside myself that may have always been there: my "inner toolkit."

Frankly, I don't know if my inner toolkit is real or not. But I do know that for the first time in my life, I began to feel a sense of capability and resourcefulness. I felt that if I needed a capability, I could reach inside myself, grab it, and put it to good use. I almost felt like Neo in *The Matrix*, receiving a downloaded capability whenever I needed it. In reality, my capabilities were probably always there, waiting to be tapped, but I never pushed myself hard enough to discover them. Chances are, I was caught up too deeply in my victim mindset and playing too much defense to realize the capabilities I always had at my disposal.

I would love to tell you that I made up the term "inner toolkit," but it's certainly not original. I first heard it from Rabbi David Begoun in a thoughtful lecture he gave many years before I started my improvement. The term intrigued me then, but I didn't give it much thought until years later when I started to improve my speech and feel a new sense of resourcefulness.

My inner toolkit was a treasure trove of capabilities that propelled me well beyond what I thought possible. I discovered a new capacity for resourcefulness, persistence, drive, and creativity. Not sure how to handle the pressure of a challenging question from a client, I reached into my inner toolkit and realized that I didn't have to jump to attention and answer right away—I could pause, formulate a thoughtful answer, take a full breath, and speak deliberately. Falling apart when speaking with authority figures, I turned to humor, expressiveness, and having fun to defuse my tension and even the playing field. Feeling time pressure in talking, I decided to resist that trap, recognizing that I could only speak well when going at my own pace. I wasn't always successful the first time, but with consistency and enough reps, I eventually was able to work through these and other stuttering challenges. In retrospect, many of these were cases of doing the opposite, but still, I felt like I was tapping into a creative vein of solutions that once seemed beyond my capacity. As I climbed my hierarchy, challenges arose, and somehow, I found answers. This was new.

All of these successes led to a can-do feeling that blew away my previous conception of myself. Previously I felt trapped by my stuttering; now I felt resourceful, believing I could handle whatever challenge came my way. I could think on my feet, ideas flowed freely from mind to mouth. The deeper I reached into my toolkit, the more goodies I found. I routinely came up with ideas to address my stuttering that I had never considered.

After a lifetime of muddling aimlessly with stuttering, I don't know how a stream of ideas suddenly began to flow into my mind, such as taking small steps, creating a hierarchy, thinking opposite/doing opposite, and breaking the anticipation cycle. Once I started to see some progress, new ideas seemed to spring up on demand, pushing me to experiment with these concepts. If necessity is the mother of invention, I know exactly where that mother stores her tools—the same place we all do—inside her inner toolkit.

Building Confidence That Lasts

After a lifetime of wishing and hoping for better speech and getting nowhere, taking small steps and stacking one small success after another was having a massive impact on my speech. Small successes were piling up like bricks in a building, becoming my foundation and source of confidence. The progress seemed real, and so did my gain in confidence.

At this point, what was success? No, it wasn't necessarily perfectly fluent speech. Rather, it was the confidence to speak at will, to not hold back, and to say what I wanted. Sure, I was still stuttering here and there, though much less than in the past. More importantly, I wasn't avoiding speaking situations; now, I was grabbing every speaking opportunity I could. Taking the offensive, I ventured forth in the world as a confident speaker, taking on challenges that once paralyzed me—but always one small step at a time.

In business meetings, I now had the confidence to move from small talk to the big talk that wins new accounts, such as asking difficult questions; answering a prospect's challenging queries with strong, confident responses; and asking for a million dollars to open a new account. This was huge for me, making me feel like I was finally able to build my business and go after new business like a real investment advisor rather than one with his hands tied behind his back. I came out of the back room and into the fray. On a personal level, I now had the confidence to be fully engaged in conversational back and forth, with no holding back, no parsing of words. I could say exactly what I wanted to say, ushering in a new and unexpected sense of freedom.

Success was becoming an expectation, a habit. I even began to call it the success habit. Stacking successes as I climbed higher and higher in my hierarchy of steps, I felt like I was knocking down doors. I took on all comers. See a challenge, take it, chalk up another win. Piling up successes in rapid succession, I was bursting with confidence. My newfound freedom in speaking was liberating, empowering.

I felt good—better than good. I felt unstoppable. I was seeking out challenges; I couldn't get enough. I felt a mastery that was entirely new to me. This wasn't the flimsy, momentary confidence born from positive thinking that falls away when the going gets tough. No, this was earned confidence. True confidence. The real thing. Nothing could stop me now. Not a disappointment. Not a bad day. Nothing. I was there. That's how I built true confidence, the kind that lasts, one small step at a time.

Was I Finally Ready?

For months, I progressed through my hierarchy, climbing my ladder of stuttering challenges. It felt great. I was confident, capable, and resourceful, working through whatever challenges came my way. Reaching into my inner toolkit, I found that one solution seemed to lead to another.

There was just one more step to take: to say my name and introduce myself. It haunted me all my life. Here I was, fifty-seven years old, finally facing my menace like the young sheriff squaring off against the legendary gunslinger in the middle of Main Street. This was not the first time I tried to face this challenge, not by a long shot, but it was definitely the first time that I thought I had a chance at success. For once in my life, I thought I had done the work, had a strategy, and was ready to finally put this bogey behind me.

Why was it so hard to say my name? Maybe because it's a personal representation of who I am? Or because I couldn't substitute words—my name is my name, and I couldn't get around those two words? Yes, I admit it: There were times when I thought of changing my name, as some people who stutter have done. Saying my name was like being backed into a corner. There were no choices, no easy exits. I had to say those two words, nothing else would do. There was no way out.

I always struggled terribly trying to say my name, and there had never been a time when I didn't. Not even once. First, I couldn't get out the L in Larry, then the St in Stein. I have no idea how long it usually took me to say my name, maybe around fifteen seconds or so. But it always felt a lot longer, maybe a minute or two, maybe a lifetime. During those fifteen seconds, it seemed as if I were projected into a slow-motion reality that stretched on forever. By the time I made it through my name, I was exhausted, as if I had gone through a gauntlet.

So many times, that one simple, unassuming question threw me into pure panic: What's your name? My Disneyland experience was just one of a zillion; it happened all the time. It seemed like every new experience in life started with that question and ended with the same result. There was no end to the nightmare, from the first day of school or camp, to the first week of classes in college, to the first day of a new job, to introductions at the beginning of business meetings or on the phone. It was no different introducing myself in a business meeting at age fifty-five than on the first day of kindergarten at age five. It was always the same.

It was even more embarrassing to go through this as an adult. Little kids can say their names, why can't I? So many times, I found myself stuck in a conference room, my anxiety rising as fellow professionals went around the room calmly introducing themselves, often with an ingratiating smile. One by one, I counted down the people until it would be my turn, and it was kindergarten all over again. The result was always the same: LLLLLLLLLLLLarry StStSttttttein. Brutal. Exhausting. Fifty years may have passed, but nothing was different. It was always the same story, the same nightmare. I hadn't grown a bit. When would it end?

Maybe now? Was I finally ready? I had come so far in my journey, handling challenges and building confidence well beyond any previous expectation. And yet, despite those successes, saying my name seemed different, maybe even insurmountable. On the other hand, I would never be done with stuttering until I was done with my name. It was time.

Taking On the Challenge of My Life

I was committed to approaching my name as I had every challenge before it: one small step at a time. By now, I was comfortable in just about every speaking situation I could find, but somehow, this was different. Intellectually, it shouldn't have been. I was trying to convince myself that my name was just another two-word phrase, no different from any other, just another pair of widgets. While this surely made intellectual sense, my mind wasn't buying it. There was too much history, too much trauma. Despite my rationalizations, it was much more than just another small step or another phrase—it was the challenge of my life. I had to mount an all-out effort. I had to win.

To face this challenge, I created a separate hierarchy of steps. For months, I had been laying the groundwork. As usual, I started with the easiest step: introducing myself to little kids, then moved on to other easy situations. If I were at a business meeting with a name tag on my lapel, I would introduce myself to everyone I could. They already knew my name—it was on my name tag—I used times like these as low-pressure ways to get practice in saying my name and score tons of wins. I figured the more times I said my name in easy situations, the better. I loaded up on reps; I couldn't get enough. I even called businesses and introduced myself to people who wouldn't care what my name was—hotels, restaurants, stores—anyone who would answer a phone.

For example, I would call a hardware store: "Hi, I'm Larry Stein. Do you have a hammer?" Of course, they had a hammer! What hardware store wouldn't? I did the same thing with hotels: "Hi, I'm Larry Stein. Do you have a room?" Of course, a two-thousand-room hotel had a room! That didn't matter to me: I was in it for the reps. I'm sure the person answering the phone couldn't care less about my name, and that was the point: To introduce myself with nothing riding on the outcome. No stakes whatsoever. Make it as easy as possible. There was absolutely no purpose to these introductions other than to wear down decades of fear and failure, build confidence, and get myself prepared for prime-time introductions that would actually matter.

By the time I was ready to start introducing myself for real, I had already introduced myself a zillion times in a variety of low-pressure situations. I thought I was ready.

Ironically, I found the perfect venue to take this next step due to the terribly unfortunate death of my treasured friend, Rabbi Reuven Frankel. He and I had a wonderful friendship, but he was more than a friend; he was an inspiration who continues to inspire me to this day. About six months after he passed away, his lovely wife, Penina, who also became a close and treasured friend, left town for the winter. I told Penina that while she was away, I would look for another synagogue, and to my surprise, I found one after a few weeks of attending their services.

But there was a problem: My wife didn't want to make the change yet. Why was that such a problem? Because she had always been my cover. When meeting new people, I always stood behind my wife and kids, hoping they would handle the introductions. But this time would have to be different. I wouldn't have my usual cover. Not only did my wife not go with me to the new synagogue (she did soon afterward and became very involved), but also, my kids were now adults living out of town. Losing my cover made me think twice about joining the new synagogue, but only for a moment.

By this time in my journey, I was not the same person I used to be. Taking on challenges changed me; I was growing. I thought that maybe once and for all, I was ready for this. Rather than avoid the situation as I had so many times in the past, I felt I could finally face this challenge head on. I had introduced myself so many times in so many easy situations already; it was all teed up for the real thing. At the age of fifty-seven, if I was ever going to get past this name thing, it was now.

After a ton of easy introductions to build my confidence and lay the groundwork, it was time for the next step: To introduce myself to adults in person. It seemed like the obvious next step in the progression. I had been trying out the new synagogue for a few weeks. It seemed like a good place, the right one for me. When services ended, I said to myself: "I think this is it; this is my new home. Let's make the most of it. Let's get engaged and meet everyone I can."

I cannot express how radically new this thought was for me: Not the act of joining a new place, but the idea that I would try to meet everyone I could. But that's how this last step started. That was all the planning I did: a spur-of-the-moment decision to go for it. Sure, I had laid the groundwork for months, doing a wide range of low-pressure introductions, but it was that simple decision that triggered the next and most pivotal small step of my life. I still marvel that the decision was prompted more by the desire to make a new start in a synagogue than to tackle the top of my hierarchy. I entered the social hall; scanned the room of more than 150 people milling around, eating lunch, and socializing; and got to work.

LARRY STEIN, LARRY STEIN, LARRY STEIN

I approached this challenge like any other: Start with the easiest step and work my way up. I scouted the room for the friendliest face I could find. Yes, there she was: A sweet, kind, compassionate-looking little old lady who oozed with friendliness. She was as tall as a ten-year-old, standing barely above my belt. I stepped toward her to make my first introduction, came within a few feet, then slammed on the brakes. Nope, not ready, not going to work. Even with all the work I had put in over the past months, even with all the introductions I had done in so many easy situations, even after sizing her up to be the friendliest face in the room, I still couldn't muster the confidence to move forward. This was going to be harder than I thought.

Apparently, my name was not just another two-word phrase. So much was wrapped up in those words: identity, shame, trauma, and one nightmare after another for more than fifty years. No amount of rationalization could erase those years of pain and embarrassment. Not even months of easy introductions. This was different, one of a kind. Yes, this was the top of my hierarchy.

In the past, I would have probably thrown in the towel and ended the project, but not this time, not this day. I hung in there and composed myself. *Yes, I can do this.* I searched my inner toolbox for answers. I thought I chose the friendliest face, the easiest target. And she was, but it wasn't good enough, I had to make her friendlier. Ridiculously friendly. I pictured warm rays of light emanating from her face, graced with a lovely smile. I basked in her warmth, friendly as friendly could be. It felt right.

I turned back around to her, smiled, and reached out my hand. "I don't think we've met. I'm Larry Stein." Done! I was fifty-seven years old, and for the first time in my life, I had willingly introduced myself to an adult. Wow, incredible. I did it!

Okay, so I caved in at the last second and unexpectedly snuck in a filler phrase—"I don't think we've met"—but I did it! This was fantastic; I had to double down. The filler phrase took me by surprise.

Maybe it was nervousness that led me to blurt out the phrase, but I didn't want to take the time to think about it and stop the momentum. I searched the room for the next friendliest face, basked in her glow, and introduced myself. Again success! I kept going. I couldn't stop. That day, I introduced myself to seven or more of the friendliest faces in the room, all older women. I always found it easier to speak with women; I'm not sure why. It didn't matter; I was on my way.

That week, I continued to look for easy situations to introduce myself in preparation for next Saturday's luncheon at the synagogue. Saturday came, and once again, after services, I scoured the room for the friendliest female faces I could find. I used my imagination to make them even more friendly, basked in their glow, and scored another bunch of successful introductions, first to older women, then to women around my age. Sure, I was still using the filler phrase, "I don't think we've met," but the introductions flowed easier and easier as the day progressed. This was exciting.

Fear was giving way to confidence. Introducing myself to women around my age was an important step, but there was still one more to go, and frankly, it was more than just another small step: To introduce myself to men. That would be the real test, maybe the last step of my entire hierarchy. The third Saturday came. Services ended and I knew what I had to do. I warmed up with a few introductions to women; easy peasy, no hesitation at all, though I still used the filler phrase without planning to—it just kept on coming out that way. Nonetheless, I thought I was ready.

If I was ever going to take that last small step, this was it. The time was now. I looked for the friendliest male face I could find: a short, old man barely up to my shoulders. I imagined the warm rays and the comforting smile. I felt the warmth, smiled, and went for my first introduction. Success! Sure, I snuck in the "I don't think we've met" line again before my name, but it was a success, nonetheless. Count it! I looked for the next candidate and scored again! And again! I couldn't stop, though I was running out of older men for introductions.

It was time for the last small step of all my small steps: To introduce myself to men my own age. This was it, the top of my hierarchy. I looked around the room and took my first shot: "I don't think we've met. I'm Larry Stein." Success! Scored another success, another, and another after that. I turned toward a distinguished man in a $3,000 suit, reached out my hand, smiled, and simply said, "Larry Stein." And to another, "Larry Stein." And another, "Larry Stein." No filler words, no lead up. Just me: Larry Stein. Nothing more. I didn't need anything more; it was done.

Free at Last

I know it's a cliché, but I actually felt it: I felt the weight of the world fall from my shoulders. The sun shined. Birds sang. My mouth fell slack as decades of tension melted away, maybe even remnants dating back to my childhood. It was done. I was fifty-seven, and for the first time in my life, I was free.

I thought being able to say my name would be my greatest challenge, but I had no idea how pivotal it would be. Saying my name changed everything for me. It was the release of fifty years of anxiety, the shift from fear and avoidance to calm and confidence. There was no longer any need to hide or any reason to be on high alert. I could say anything; I could just be me. It was as if the world flung its doors wide open and all I could see was green—pure opportunity stretched as far as I could see. Now, nothing was out of reach.

For once, I was free. Free to speak, free to do as I wished. The chains were broken, the shell was shattered. It was just one small step, yet so monumental and life-changing. An ethereal calm washed over me, and the mental machinations dissolved, falling away like melting snow.

Now I could see how hiding from stuttering permeated every aspect of my life. I could also see the staggering costs involved, well beyond anything I could have possibly imagined. But I accepted all of that; the past was in the past. The future was laid out like a red carpet, inviting me to step forward and see what's next.

Ironically, I was left with less than when the journey started. The veils were gone. The masks, the false bravado: gone. It was all gone. I was stripped bare, left with nothing more than who I am. I experienced a lot of surprises in my stuttering journey, but this was one of the most striking: To be the real me. It was as if I were reborn.

You're Never Really Done

Once I climbed to the top of my hierarchy and was able to say my name, I thought I was done. I could now do the one thing that had plagued me my entire life; I didn't have to hide from anyone or any speaking situation. I didn't have to hide from life. I was free. I felt empowered to build my business and develop new personal relationships. I was changed.

I had my moment in the sun; now, I thought I could sit back and relax. I was wrong. Even after the weight of the world fell from my shoulders, the sun shined and birds sang, there were still aspects of my stuttering that needed to be addressed. I noticed that I still sometimes had difficulty at the beginning of sentences, asking questions, introducing others, and breaking into group conversations.

At first, I was a bit miffed by this unfinished business. I had had my triumphant moment, and I wanted to ride off into the sunset. It wasn't to be. Not yet, at least. Fortunately, I was able to work through the remaining difficulties with strategies I had already developed. Though I initially resented the need for additional work, I have to admit that I enjoyed the experience. I found it exciting to work through the more complex riddles of my stuttering, test strategies, put them into practice, and celebrate new triumphs.

For me, now, challenges are no longer something to be feared and avoided; they're part of the pavement of my life. They're the bumps in the road I have to travel, I want to travel. No bumps, no learning, no triumphs. I'm not looking for new bumps, that's for sure. But if they arise, I feel confident that I now have a process to work through them, at least to some extent.

So, am I done? No, not at all. Probably never will be. I still occasionally have nightmares about stuttering: saying my name, and other situations. And I wake up, wondering for a moment whether stuttering will one day overtake me again. The honest answer is that I don't think so, but I can't be entirely sure. It's been ten years since I was finally able to say my name, but you never know. With the Covid pandemic, I haven't been engaged in as many speaking situations as I would like. My speaking machine is a bit rusty, and my confidence isn't as rock-solid as it had been. I'm pretty sure that stuttering is now in my rearview mirror, but not as sure as I once was. Even now, reps are important; I need to keep reinforcing. You're never really done.

Challenges continue to arise now and then, daring me to address them. Whether it's stuttering or something else, I still need to steel myself sometimes, reach into my inner toolkit, and work through the challenge du jour. The challenges never end, nor do they seem to go away completely. Occasionally, minor remnants rear their head, doubts arise. I sometimes have to remind myself about all the good things in my life and that it's not all about facing challenges, which have, fortunately, become a much, much smaller part of my entirety.

Still, the beat goes on; there will always be something. In a sense, I'm thankful for the work left undone. Unlike when I was younger and less capable, I now relish working through the mysteries of new challenges. I love the uncertainty, the process, the juice. Challenges generate growth. They test my mettle, keep me sharp, and focus my attention. Even at sixty-seven, I'm still a work in progress; the growth goes on. May it never stop.

Section 4:
Insights

THAT'S MY STORY. I've given you all I can, as well as I can remember. But the story doesn't end there. I continue to learn more, both from mentoring others and dealing with my own moments of minor disfluency, which, thankfully, are pretty rare. Now that you've read my story, here are the most impactful insights I've learned in this journey.

There Is Always a Way Forward

Facing stuttering is such a daunting process; I found it so hard to get started. For me, stuttering was a massive monolith, seemingly unapproachable, impossible to penetrate. It blocked the light. I stuttered for fifty years. Stuttering was who I was. It defined me. It seeped into every thought and action I had. How could I possibly change my speech after so many years and such a deep impact? For decades, I couldn't see a solution; I couldn't see a way forward. I gave up and wallowed in the muck, struggling to make it through life.

You may feel that way, too. Your situation may seem desperate, maybe even impossible. But here's what I've learned: You may think you've reached a dead end, that it's over. But it's not—not unless you give up and shut the door completely. It's entirely up to you: Your situation won't shut the door, only you can. Otherwise, there's always hope. There is always a way forward.

If there is one thing I have learned in my stuttering journey, it's this: There may not be a solution, but there is always a way forward.

How can I be so certain?

Because I struggled with stuttering for fifty years. I did everything wrong you can imagine. I compromised my career, shied away from social situations, and passed on potentially rewarding career opportunities, all to avoid stuttering. All I got from it was terrible frustration and debilitating depressions. I knew I was wasting my life. But I didn't know what else to do. I was resigned to a life ruled by stuttering.

Then things changed. Desperate to build my business, I began to take action with my speech. I started small, saw some early progress, and felt encouraged enough to push the rock forward. One small success led to another, and soon I was hooked; I didn't want to stop. I grew to relish the challenge and find joy in each small success. I knew there was no solution to my stuttering, but there was a way forward, and it proved to be more rewarding and thrilling than I could have possibly imagined.

For me, the way forward was like the "Thrilla in Manilla" fight in 1975 between Joe Frazier and Muhammad Ali. Frazier kept coming at Ali, one step at a time, taking on an inhumane barrage of punches. But Frazier kept coming and eventually prevailed. That's how my journey was with stuttering: I just kept coming, one small step at a time, fighting my way through speaking challenges. It was hard and always uncertain, but ultimately exhilarating. It was the battle of my life, my signature victory.

I often look back at my life in disbelief. How could I have made so many mistakes over the years, and yet, I've achieved the two goals I had in life: to be able to speak confidently and to run my own investment firm. And then I went beyond those two goals to do something even more meaningful: to help others with their speech. It's still hard for me to believe. Here I am at sixty-seven, profoundly grateful for what I have and looking forward to grabbing every bit of life I can in the years I have left. At a time when many of my friends are retiring or contemplating it, in many ways, my life is just beginning. I am finally free to speak, and I want to see how far I can go with it.

Maybe you've gone through more than I have—perhaps a lot more. But I've gone through enough to know this: There is always a way forward. There is never a dead end unless you give up. Don't let that happen. Take that first small step, stack small successes, and find your way forward. You never know where it can lead you.

Say "Yes" to Speaking; Say "Yes" to Life

Before I found my way forward, "no" was my default response to speaking, my default response to life. No was easy. It eliminated stress and responsibility. The more I said no, the less I spoke, and that made life a lot easier for me.

But saying no was a trap. It kept me under the thumb of stuttering. By saying no, I was able to avoid speaking opportunities, but it left me with so few moments of talking that each one became a monumental event filled with anxiety. Saying no also caused me to miss out on a lot in life, from career opportunities to social enjoyment. I can't imagine how different my life would be today if, right from the start, I said yes rather than no. Stuttering didn't have to be the determinant of my life; I could have stuttered heavily and still said yes. But I didn't.

Fortunately, in the past decade, I found my way forward and gained the confidence to say yes. As a result, I've caught up with much of what I missed, though certainly not everything—there are some experiences that cannot be recovered. They're lost forever. Saying yes is the road to happiness; saying no is the path to regrets. You don't want regrets; they will gnaw at you mercilessly.

Saying no had another impact: It kept me in a victim mindset, feeling sorry for myself. "Why me? Why do I have to stutter?" Soon after I started my all-out effort to improve my speech, I realized that I was never going to reach my goals if I had a victim mindset. I also was never going to fully enjoy life, either. That had to change. I had to say yes.

Say yes to speaking, yes to opportunities, yes to responsibility, yes to life. It's much harder to say yes, to take on the responsibility of handling life's ups and downs. Responsibilities challenge you to learn and grow, to handle life's uncertainties and trying moments, and to experience failure and grow from it. For years, I hid from responsibility. As a result, I had serious deficits in my maturity, resilience, and capabilities. After I started saying yes, it took me years to catch up and be able to handle the responsibilities of life. There were times in my late fifties when I felt like a teenager, still working through the basics of life, trying to find my way. Now, at sixty-seven, I think I'm just about there.

The impact of saying yes was life-changing. By saying yes to speaking opportunities and yes to life, I gradually moved from the sidelines to fully engaging in the fray, with all the opportunities, responsibilities, and difficult moments that go along with it. Sometimes the transition wasn't easy; I stumbled a lot. But I finally took responsibility for those stumbles and grew in the process.

Sure, saying yes created a more challenging life, but it also led me to experience more of the joys. Frankly, I'm thankful for both; I have grown from the challenges, and I relish the joys. Both are essentials of a life well-lived. Take the chance: Say yes. You'll feel more pain and experience more failure, but you'll also live more fully and grow. Take the chance; it's worth it.

Insights

Don't Let Stuttering Compromise You

One of the main reasons I wrote this book is to warn others not to make the same mistake I did: to avoid stuttering so much that I compromised my life. It is perhaps my signature failure, but decades later, it became one of my most valuable learnings. Don't compromise your life for anything, especially for stuttering. Don't let that happen to you; rise above it.

Stuttering didn't have to stop me. I could have risen above it like so many others. Now that I have become involved in the stuttering world, I am amazed to see so many people who stutter have highly successful careers. They are much more courageous than I was, and I admire them greatly. I have met successful people who stutter in medicine, law, business, academia, engineering, and the arts. At the time of this writing, the president of the United States (Joe Biden) still occasionally displays remnants of his childhood stutter. Stuttering shouldn't limit any dream you have or any career you choose, nor should you let it.

Perhaps the most common question I get from high school and college students who stutter is, "Do you think I could become a _____ (doctor, lawyer, businessperson, etc.), even though I stutter?" My answer is clear and resounding: "Of course you can, as long as you're willing to put in the work. Your stuttering may make your path a bit more challenging, particularly at the beginning of your career, but if you work hard enough, your competence will speak for itself. Don't let stuttering hold you back from anything you want to do. Nothing is out of your reach."

In truth, stuttering didn't get in the way of my dreams—I did. It was all me. I could have worked harder and been more courageous in forging ahead with my career. I could have filled my college and graduate school career with so many accomplishments that some investment firm would have hired me, even with my stuttering. Compromising my career had very little to do with my stuttering; it was much more about me—my lack of will to make my dreams happen.

Stuttering is not an excuse; I made it an excuse. As a result, I paid a heavy price: regret, unhappiness, and depression. I nearly paid the ultimate price. Don't let that happen to you. Sure, your stuttering may present a speed bump now and then, but don't let anything hold you back, especially yourself. Find your way forward and make it happen.

Think You're Not Ready? Think Again!

As you read this book, you may think, "Wow, it sounds so hard to work through stuttering. I don't think I can do it. I don't have the inner strength, the drive, the persistence. I can't do this. I'm not ready." You may think all those things, and you might be right. You might not be ready to work through your stuttering, at least not right now. But that's okay.

Neither was I. Not at all. I was a classic underperformer, the guy who never lived up to his potential. I'd start strong with amped-up

Insights

enthusiasm, then give up when I'd hit a bump in the road. Sure, I had some drive, but I lacked the inner strength and persistence to move the needle and sustain the effort. I lacked follow-through. So, how did I work through my stuttering? What was different this time? I sensed a little bit of progress that seemed real and thought I could build on it. One success led to another, and soon I was hooked.

With each small step, each small success, my confidence grew. And so did I. Those first small successes felt so good that I didn't want them to end. Fear gave way to confidence, propelling me up my hierarchy to heights I could never have imagined. All the way to today.

As you can see, initially I wasn't ready either. But in hindsight, that was okay. Maybe even necessary. Maybe it had to be that way to push me on to greater heights, to be willing to try anything and fail before finding my next step forward. I didn't have to be perfect; I just had to stick with it and keep pushing ahead.

It didn't matter that I wasn't ready, because I changed, I grew. The process changed me. I became more resourceful, persistent, and resilient. The first small success started changing me, and I'm still changing today. The process keeps pushing forward, and I continue to discover new things about myself, who I am, and what I can be.

So, if you don't think you're ready to take on your stuttering, think again. In fact, don't think at all. Just start. Take your first small step, score your first small success, and keep pushing forward. Let the process take you. Enjoy the ride.

Focus on What Matters

Like a magician pulling our eyes to irrelevant motion, stuttering leads us to focus on the wrong things. One of the more common questions I hear is, "What is the cause of my stuttering?" My answer is straightforward: "I have no idea." The question makes sense and is well-intentioned, but frankly, it's probably unknowable, irrelevant, and a waste of time. Does it really matter? Is it going to help you improve your speech? I've paid so much money to so many types of therapists in trying to figure out my life and never got anywhere. Even if I got somewhere in terms of understanding, would it have helped my speech?

Even more than the "why" question, stuttering pulls our focus to one thing: fluency. Everybody wants to be fluent; I certainly did. That's all I wanted. But it's a trap, don't fall for it. Making fluency the measuring stick of your life will only frustrate you, especially in the early stages of trying to improve your speech. It's not realistic. An all-or-nothing goal of being fluent is a harsh burden to place on yourself. Let it go. Set realistic goals, not one that requires you to score 100 percent every time you speak.

The fluency trap can also create an unhealthy focus on the self. This can sabotage efforts to improve your speech. Questions overload your mind, such as, "Oh no, I think I'm going to stutter! What will the other person think? How can I get around this stutter? Should I say this word or maybe that one? Should I even talk at all?" The mind twists at the mercy of the stuttering hurricane, trying to make sense of the insanity. You can't win this.

Instead, my experience has taught me to view fluency as an afterthought, a byproduct of the progress you make with your speech. Fluency is the result of what you do. In my case, what I did was relearn to speak, retrain my brain, and work through my hierarchy of speaking challenges in small steps. I felt that if I worked hard and did the right things, some measure of fluency would follow. And it did, much more than I thought possible.

Communication is not a test of fluency; it's how we humans connect with each other. Rather than seeing how little you can stutter, focus on the connection: Was it meaningful, impactful, enjoyable? That's what really counts. You can't win the self-scrutiny game. You'll always strike out in one sense or another.

Don't get caught in the fluency trap. Do the opposite: Place your focus on the other person and see how much you can give and enjoy—you'll be much happier and your speech may improve in the process. Set a goal to enjoy every conversation, regardless of the content or context, and give whatever you can to the other person. Give and enjoy. Take the focus off yourself and give, give, give.

Make Speaking Routine, Not a Test

I've learned a lot from mentoring people who stutter. One of the most important insights is to realize how absolutely essential it is to talk with others throughout your day, every day. The more, the better. Many people who stutter don't talk enough, and frankly, for years, neither did I. As you just read, my default response to speaking and just about everything else was "no." But talking is imperative. You can't improve your speech without immersing yourself in live speaking situations. You've got to get out there and talk so much that it becomes routine.

Here's why: If you have too few speaking opportunities, it's easy to fall into the trap of viewing every conversation as a test of whether you stuttered or not. As a result, speaking becomes a pressure-packed event filled with crippling anxiety. That's destructive on many levels. It needlessly magnifies the importance of each speaking situation and raises the stakes for fluency—both are destructive. Why should speaking be a test? Doesn't that put too much stress on yourself? Yes, it does. I know that firsthand.

Getting more involved in the work world changed things for me. Speaking was no longer an event; I had to talk as part of my job, and my speech improved. Not from therapy, not from strategy, but just from sheer reps in talking. Even though I took jobs in accounting and at NICOR to avoid having to talk much on the job, there was enough speaking involved to have a positive impact on my speech. When I took the job at FRB and had to talk throughout my day in meetings and on the phone, my speech improved significantly. Talking so much wore down my fears and, in a sense, trivialized speaking. Talking was no longer a big deal; it was routine, and that was good.

The work world is one of the best places to make speaking routine. Work environments are filled with a wide variety of speaking opportunities, with people milling around and socializing, coworkers dropping in, casual conversations, phone calls, and meetings. The variety and frequency are great for improving your speech. Unfortunately, in today's digital world, especially during the recent Covid pandemic, it's now easier than ever to hide and avoid speaking. Don't let that happen to you. Fight it. Do whatever you can to get involved with others and talk, talk, talk.

You can learn every strategy I discuss in this book, and it won't make a bit of difference unless you reinforce it with constant conversation in the real world. No amount of positive thinking and self-acceptance will do. Even hours and hours of well-intentioned practice by yourself won't move the needle. You've got to get out there and talk so much that it becomes routine. The constant talking I did in the work world and, especially, in running my own business turned speaking from a high-anxiety event into one of the most fun and relaxing things I do.

Don't hide like I did. Get out there and talk as much as you can, both in your personal life and in your work. Speaking should not be a test nor an event; it's how you connect with others and enjoy their company. Change the paradigm from an anxiety-producing test to a daily source of enjoyment. Make it routine; make it fun.

Own It: My Michael Jordan Rule

Throughout my stuttering life, I used any possible excuse to rationalize why I had a "bad stuttering day." My excuses were endless, including these ridiculous ones: "I have a cold, a bad haircut, or new clothes that make me self-conscious," and so on. Anytime I needed an out, I always had one at the ready. There was no limit to the rationalizations or their implausibility, yet I held on to them for dear life.

Why were excuses such a problem? Because I didn't own up to the challenge and I didn't take responsibility for my stuttering. As long as I was willing to accept excuses for stuttering, I was free from the responsibility to improve my speech.

Then along came Michael Jordan. That's right, the basketball player. Let me set the scene: June 11, 1997, game five of the NBA Finals between the Chicago Bulls and the Utah Jazz. The series is tied two-to-two, and Michael Jordan shows up at the game in Utah with what the media originally reported as "flu-like symptoms." Jordan struggled in the first quarter, and the Jazz built a sixteen-point lead. It looked bad for the Bulls. Then Jordan took over. In the second quarter, he scored seventeen points en route to a thirty-eight-point, seven-rebound game. He led the Bulls to a 90–88 victory, hitting a three-pointer with less than a minute left to seal the win. The Bulls won the game and later the series, all thanks to Michael Jordan's iconic performance. He took responsibility for his team and carried them on his back, even though he was so sick he needed to be helped off the court. Whether he had the flu (as initially reported) or food poisoning (as some later believed), it was a heroic performance for the ages, widely known as the "flu game."

It also became a heroic model for me. Some fifteen years later, I would look back on this performance and create my Michael Jordan Rule: There is never an excuse for my stuttering. If I stutter, I stutter; that's okay, it's mine, I'm doing it. But there is never an excuse; it's always me. There is no such thing as a "bad stuttering day." Stuttering doesn't happen to me; I'm the one who stutters. The responsibility for my speech is all mine. Period. I own it.

This was one of the most important mindset changes I made in my entire journey: to take responsibility for my speech. I would no longer look for an excuse, a rationalization, or a way out. No, it's me. All me. I'm the one stuttering, and I'm the one who needs to take responsibility for improving my speech. There's no magic cure, no easy way out—it's all up to me.

Taking responsibility for my stuttering and the improvement of my speech spurred me on to become more resourceful. There were no excuses anymore; it was my responsibility to keep progressing toward my goal. If I was stymied by a challenge in working through a rung in my speaking hierarchy, I tapped my inner toolkit, searched for a way forward, and did my best to make it a success. And if it didn't go well, that was okay, I could always try again. Like Michael Jordan, nothing was going to stop me from my goal, at least not a flimsy excuse. From that point on, my stuttering was mine; I owned it, for better or worse.

Start with a Solid Foundation: BEP

One of the most common questions I hear is: "Do you have any tips, tricks, and techniques to become fluent?" No, I don't. I do not believe in any of those. They're short-term fixes that may give you a momentary bump in fluency, but they won't have a long-term impact, and, to me, the long term is all that matters.

To change your speech for the long term, you need a strategy that:

1. Makes sense

2. Is used all the time

3. You have made automatic

Let's go through these points one at a time.

BEP makes sense because it's how good speakers speak. It's natural. It's not robotic or stilted. President Joe Biden doesn't use BEP, but in interviews, he has said that he marks up his speeches with slashes to break the text into what seems like phrases. Professional speakers speak in phrases to make their delivery more compelling and help their audience digest their messages. The shorter the phrases, the more powerful the delivery, the easier to digest.

I didn't invent BEP; I just mimicked Matt Lauer and other broadcasters and simplified their speaking to three basic elements: Breathe, Emphasize, Phrase. Then I learned that BEP is much more effective if I am as expressive as possible, which creates constant airflow that recirculates like a fountain. Being expressive and emphasizing words use up your breath, so you can take a fresh, full breath to begin each phrase. I pictured my breathing like a sine wave, going up and down in cycles, one phrase at a time. This creates rhythmic, flowing speech. It's a wonderful feeling, almost intoxicating—you may not want to stop talking.

Speaking in phrases breaks down a massive problem—stuttering—into one phrase at a time. Chances are, you've been taking a similar approach to handling problems all your life, whether it's building models, baking cakes, or doing math problems. It's all the same: break big problems into little steps. BEP makes sense: it's how good speakers speak, and it breaks stuttering down to one phrase at a time, one breath per phrase.

To take that breath, you need to do something that may sound crazy to a person who stutters: You need to pause in between the phrases long enough to take a full breath. Otherwise, your phrases won't be distinct; they'll run together, and it won't really be phrasing at all. Pausing creates the phrase and gives you time to breathe in between. Usually, stuttering dictates breathing. We expect a stutter, hesitate, try to breathe, and do anything else to avoid the stutter. It's a losing battle. Don't let stuttering take control of your breathing; you take control. You decide when to breathe, how to use up your breath with emphasis and expressiveness, and when to end the phrase. You take control, one phrase at a time.

Let me address the second point by answering another common question I hear: "When should I use BEP?" The answer is simple: All the time. Don't think you can pull BEP out of your pocket when you need it—that's unrealistic, and it will fail. BEP only has value if you use it all the time. This necessitates a difficult decision for most people: You have to be willing to give up your old way of speaking. Get rid of it entirely. There can be no half-measures; you've got to go all in. And that means BEP must be the only way you speak, period. Frankly, this will come down to discipline: Making the decision to speak with BEP all the time in every situation, no matter if the situation is hard or easy, hurried or not. All the time.

Third, BEP will only be effective if it is so automatic that you don't think about it, that it's as natural as breathing. This will take a ton of reps, but it's the only way forward. If BEP is not automatic, then it's just another technique, and all techniques are bound to fail when the pressure is on. People who stutter know this: When the pressure to speak is on, everything goes out the window and it's impossible to think—that's why BEP has to be automatic so you don't have to think about it. Once BEP is automatic, it's no longer a technique, it's a part of you. Make it yours.

Remember, BEP is not your ticket to fluency. By itself, BEP may have brought me perhaps halfway to my speaking goals, probably less. But its importance is clear: Without making BEP automatic, I would never have made such an improvement in my speech. BEP was the foundation for everything I did. It made everything possible.

Break Your Stuttering Inclinations

Once I became proficient at BEP and made it automatic, I was surprised to realize that speaking mechanics were only the starting point of my improvement. In fact, BEP proved to be the easy part: it's mainly a matter of brute-force to learn it, use it in the real world, and make it automatic.

Then something completely unexpected happened. As the climb up my hierarchy became more challenging and I ran into roadblocks, I was struck by the realization that fifty years of stuttering really messed me up, leaving me with an untold number of what I eventually called "stuttering inclinations." These inclinations were a complex web of psychological impacts that seemed to rule my speech and my overall thought process. I had no idea how to address these inclinations, but I knew that I couldn't reach my goals without working through their riddles.

One of the most common stuttering inclinations is the anticipation cycle, and I spun in this insidious loop for decades. It dominated my thinking, trying to anticipate which words or sounds I might stutter on before actually saying them. This led to endless calculations on how I could avoid stuttering, pushing my brain into a frenzied overdrive. There were a seemingly endless number of other stuttering inclinations, such as avoiding speaking situations, avoiding people, rationalizing why I didn't want to speak with certain people, shortening my speaking time to the bare minimum, holding on so tight to avoid stuttering that I became rigid and nearly unable to function, and agreeing to do things I abhorred rather than explain why I wouldn't, among others.

My desperation to break these inclinations led me to another Hail Mary strategy: Do the opposite. It was so radical, so ridiculous, that I almost laughed the first time I tried it. By doing the opposite, I gradually broke one stuttering inclination after another. For example, rather than avoid, I engaged. Rather than convey a thought in as few words as possible, I lengthened my words well beyond the necessary length. Instead of anticipating a stutter, I learned to trust my ability to execute BEP, say exactly what I wanted, and let the chips fall where they may. Sure, I stuttered more, but it was one moment in time rather than succumbing to a lifetime of fear. The stuttering anticipation cycle came down to a choice: avoid words and stutter heavily forever, or give myself a chance to improve my speech by risking stuttering and saying exactly what I wanted. Ironically, stuttering proved to be the way to improvement.

Rather than feed inclinations by giving in to them, I starved them by doing the opposite. Recognizing an inclination in mid-form, I would stop the cycle and question, "What would be the opposite?" Then I did it. I don't think anyone noticed my real-time self-therapy in action, but I didn't care—I could sense the gradual positive impact it was having on my speech. The world was my laboratory, and doing the opposite was my go-to strategy for change.

Years later, I would learn that doing the opposite is a well-established strategy in Cognitive Behavioral Therapy. I stumbled upon it, the product of desperation. You don't have to stumble; I've done that for you—try it. Make the world your laboratory, make yourself your laboratory, and have at it. Do the opposite and break your stuttering inclinations, one after another. Break, break, break. Keep breaking until you uncover the real you.

Insights

True Confidence Is Earned

Everyone wants to gain confidence, but not everyone is willing to pay the price. That was me when I was younger: lots of hope and good intention, and not enough work. Positive thoughts are nice, but they only go so far. They may give you a momentary rush of confidence, but those feel-good moments are likely to slip away when the pressure is on. And there you are, back to square one.

After a lifetime of hoping for confidence and getting nowhere, I found a different way, a much slower way. Rather than rely on hope, I put in the work, one small step at a time. With each small step, each small success, green shoots of confidence began to take root. I also began to gain traction and the resilience to climb my hierarchy without suffering major setbacks along the way. No more back to square one; I was finally able to keep pushing forward, stacking one small success after another.

The brain is a tough taskmaster. It doesn't buy happy talk. You need to prove success with actual positive experiences—you've got to win over and over. Action is the brain's currency. You are what you do. If you want to change, your brain says, "Prove it. Show me what you've got." That's why small steps, stacking one small success after another in rapid succession, are so powerful. You're effectively speaking the language of change to your brain.

The importance of stacking successes in rapid succession cannot be overstated. One success is not enough to move the needle; your brain needs more. A single success will die on the vine; that feel-good moment will decay into doubt and the feeling that you got lucky.

Reinforce your success. Flood your brain with one success after another in rapid succession, and you'll feel a surge of confidence, creating a platform you can build on. Keep building. Don't let the confidence lapse.

Change is a long, slow slog. One small step at a time is the long and slow way forward, but there's joy in the slog, gratification in the work. Effort is your partner: the more you give, the more you grow. Discovering your hidden capabilities and developing new strengths are wonders of the human experience. You don't have to accept the status quo of who you are: You can change; you can grow. Too many back down from the slog. That's unfortunate because they're missing out—the long, slow slog is the gateway to real growth, both in your speech and in your life.

Confidence is the product of that growth. One small step at a time, one small success at a time, you advance toward your goal. Stack enough small successes in rapid succession, and you may find yourself gaining so much confidence that you experience what I call the "success habit," an expectation of success every time you speak. If you can climb so high that you reach the upper rungs of your hierarchy, you may find yourself bursting with confidence. You'll be knocking down doors, eating challenges for breakfast. You'll feel unstoppable, that nothing can stop you. It's not magic: You've earned it. You've built confidence one small success at a time. That's the stuff of true confidence, the kind that lasts.

Insights

Why I Succeeded This Time

After so many false starts and failed attempts to improve my speech, why did this effort succeed? It's hard to say, but I can point to at least ten factors in this attempt that may not have been present in the others. I:

1. Engaged with the world

2. Took responsibility for my stuttering

3. Made a total commitment

4. Gave up my previous way of speaking

5. Developed effective speaking mechanics

6. Broke myself by doing the opposite

7. Went small rather than going big

8. Gained confidence by stacking small successes

9. Climbed a hierarchy toward my ultimate goal

10. Grew from working through my challenges

Let's go through these factors one by one, and you'll get a better idea of why I was able to meet my goals this time. I've already touched on all these factors, but it will be helpful to see them presented here together in one place.

First, I engaged with the world.

I spent most of my life hiding from stuttering. Sure, my life seemed normal—I played sports through my younger years, went to college, got married, had kids, and held jobs. But I was always hiding from speaking, always hiding from stuttering. I hid behind my parents when I was young and hid behind my wife and kids when I was an adult. True, I worked, but I hid in jobs that I thought wouldn't involve much talking. As a result, I was chronically underemployed. Once I chose to stop hiding and to engage with the world, things changed for me. My speech improved and I enjoyed life more, too. Without taking that first step—coming out of hiding and engaging with the world—none of this would have happened. I would still be hiding and living a compromised life. Don't make that mistake. As my dad would say, "Just get out there and talk."

Second, I took responsibility for my stuttering.

One of the more common laments from people who stutter is, "I had a bad stuttering day." I must have said that a thousand times. But it's a trap. It's as if you're conceding your stuttering to an outside force that is beyond your control. It reinforces the victim mindset. When I finally realized that, I started to take responsibility for my stuttering. If I stuttered, that's fine, it's me, I own it. Once I took responsibility for my stuttering, I also began to take responsibility for my improvement. Taking responsibility for my speech became a catalyst for becoming more resourceful in finding ways to improve my speech, driving me forward toward my goals. Take responsibility for your stuttering and take action—it's all up to you.

Third, I made a total commitment.

Oddly enough, my total commitment to improving my speech only arose after I realized I would have to communicate more effectively to get more clients for my business. Otherwise, the business would fail and my family's future would be uncertain at best. My strong commitment (perhaps more accurately characterized as desperation) drove the hard work I needed in order to relearn to speak, the resourcefulness I needed to address the psychological aspects, and the persistence I needed to climb my hierarchy. Without an all-out effort, none of this would have happened; it would have been just another well-intentioned attempt like so many of my previous failures. That's what a lot of people don't realize about improving their speech: There is no easy way; there are no shortcuts. It takes a ton of work, a lot of reps, and a lot of time. You also have to be relentless and creative in working through the psychological aspects of your stuttering and the many speaking situations you've always feared. You're either all in or nothing will change.

Fourth, I gave up my previous way of speaking.

When I realized that my speech was better when I "public speak," it took me a matter of seconds to make this life-changing decision: "Why don't I just public speak all the time!" Maybe it was just desperation, but at that point, I decided to throw out my old way of speaking and move forward on this new course. That moment kickstarted my effort to improve my speech. If I didn't give up my previous way of speaking, I would never have made BEP automatic, and I would not have made such an improvement. I would still be tinkering around the edges of my stuttering, messing around with tricks and techniques, and wondering why I couldn't improve more. Sometimes you've got to give up to get where you want to go. It's not easy to give up a part of yourself, but it's an essential part of the way forward.

Fifth, I developed effective speaking mechanics.

I was never going to improve my speech with the speaking style I had—it was a mess. I needed a foundation of more effective speaking mechanics that I could rely on. The realization that my speech was better if I "public speak all the time" started the process, but at that point, I was really only phrasing. Encouraged by the improvement in my speech, I became determined to do more. I became fascinated with the speaking styles of broadcasters and mimicked them. Eventually, I simplified their speaking style to three words I could easily remember and apply: Breathe, Emphasize, Phrase (BEP). But learning BEP wasn't good enough; I soon realized that the more I thought about my speech, the more I stuttered. That led me to make BEP automatic so I didn't have to think about it. Making BEP automatic was a ton of work, but it was a game-changer, the mission-critical foundation for my improvement.

Sixth, I broke myself by doing the opposite.

Once I climbed up to the more challenging rungs of my hierarchy, something strange happened: I realized that fifty years of stuttering really messed me up. It became obvious that I had to address the psychological issues of my stuttering, what I would call my stuttering inclinations, such as avoiding speaking situations, substituting words that might cause me to stutter, or holding on so tight to keep from stuttering that I became rigid and spoke haltingly. How could I break those inclinations? By doing the opposite. Rather than avoiding, I engaged. Instead of substituting words, I said exactly what I originally intended, even if I stuttered. In place of being rigid, I played with my speech. By doing the opposite over and over, I broke my stuttering inclinations one after another. Break, break, break. By breaking myself so many times, I cleared away the clutter of my destructive stuttering inclinations, making the road to my ultimate goal possible. I had to break myself to be myself.

Seventh, I went small rather than going big.

In the past, I always tried to improve my speech by taking big, audacious leaps. When the impossible didn't happen, I usually folded and gave up. In those days, I didn't have a plan, I didn't have a strategy, and I didn't put in the work. I just wanted a miracle to happen, which is a nice intention but not enough to get me where I wanted to go. When you can't go big, go small. I went real small. I took small steps starting with the easiest possible speaking situations and stacked one small success after another. No step was a leap, just the next step in a natural progression. The more steps, the better; the easier the steps, the better. No step was too small or insignificant as long as it brought me a bit closer to my goals. There's a saying in the Talmud: "There's a shortcut that's long and a long way that's short." For once in my life, I didn't take the shortcut. I took the long way, and not only did it turn out to be short, it turned out to be sure.

***Eighth, I gained confidence
by stacking small successes.***

Confidence in my speech was always so fleeting. I would have a good day, maybe a few, and somehow feel that I was on my way. Then a single misstep would mushroom into a mess of stuttering and send me careening back to square one. I had to change that miserable loop. Taking small steps and stacking small successes one after another in rapid succession got the ball rolling toward building confidence. Going small also helped to build traction, which kept me from falling too far after setbacks. No longer was I hoping for miracles; I earned confidence the hard way, one small success at a time. After a life of feeling shreds of confidence slip through my fingers again and again, the small-step process enabled me to build true confidence, the kind that lasts.

Ninth, I climbed a hierarchy toward my ultimate goal.

Relearning to speak and addressing the psychological aspects of my stuttering were the critical building blocks of my foundation, but the real progress came from applying those building blocks and working through a hierarchy of speaking challenges in small steps. The hierarchy was dynamic: I was constantly adding new steps to make sure that no step was a leap. As I climbed the upper rungs of the hierarchy and stacked small successes, my confidence grew. Even still, it took me months to work through my ultimate goal: to be able to say my name and introduce myself. In fact, I created a separate hierarchy just for that challenge. It was a long haul, but once I finally reached the top of my hierarchy and could confidently introduce myself, life changed for me, opening up opportunities I never could have imagined.

Tenth, I grew from working through my challenges.

Working through my stuttering was a life-changing experience; I was definitely not the same person as when I started. I honestly don't know what clicked for me. Maybe I was just so desperate to save my business that I became intensely motivated to improve my speech. Perhaps I was encouraged by that first bit of improvement in my speech after I began "public speaking" all the time, and that spurred me on to further progress. I don't really know, but I know I was never so motivated, resourceful, or persistent. I had always been an underperformer, an expert at avoiding challenges. That changed as I moved through the process, eventually gaining the confidence to work through speaking situations that once paralyzed me. By challenging myself so often and in so many ways, I grew through the process, emerging as a very different person by the end of my climb. The process changed me, and I am forever thankful.

Insights

Free to Speak: How It Feels

It's been about ten years since I first felt free to speak, and I still can't believe how my life has changed. I still can't believe that I can say whatever I want regardless of the situation. Even ten years later, after a conversation ends, I still sometimes find myself expressing gratitude for my new freedom, which by now is not so new.

Being free to speak is still an amazing feeling for me. The thrill has barely worn away; it doesn't seem to get old, and I hope it never does. Situations that used to paralyze me are no longer situations at all; they're simply routine opportunities to speak, enjoy, and give. No, I'm not a perfect speaker. I still occasionally find myself aware of my speech or slip into a momentary stutter that perhaps only I can detect (perhaps not). But for the most part, stuttering is not even on my radar. I just talk. It's a feeling I never could have imagined.

Free to speak means that I can speak at will. There's no avoiding, editing, or calculating to keep from stuttering, and no questioning whether I should speak or not. My mental bandwidth is freed up, unconsumed with fears of stuttering, free to engage in whatever the moment brings. Whether it's a fun conversation, a joke, a story, a serious discussion, or a contentious exchange, my focus is on the experience and the people involved—not on my stuttering. Every conversation is an opportunity to give and enjoy.

With freedom comes calm, a feeling I had never really known. My mind is no longer racing a million miles a minute, churning desperately to figure out a way to avoid the next stutter. There's nothing to avoid. There's no need to focus on the struggle of speaking because it's no longer a struggle; my focus is on what I can give and enjoy. Calm may be a difficult concept to grasp for people who stutter—it sure was for me. It may be even harder to believe that now, the more I talk, the more calm I become. It's one of the most relaxing things I do. Oddly enough, today when I feel pressure or nervousness, I reach out for conversation—that's what calms me, that's what brings me peace.

Being free to speak changed me as a human being. After fifty years of hiding from stuttering, putting on fake smiles, and trying way too hard to offer clever banter or false bravado, I now find that I don't need those masks. I can say what I want. There's no need to hide, no need to put on an act. Stripped bare, the human being beneath all the masks is finally able to emerge. The veils are off. The veneer is gone. Peeled down to my truth, I am more grounded, more genuine, more me. The real me, I never knew. I am who I am, and that's good enough for me. I like this person.

At age sixty-seven, when many of my friends are retiring or contemplating retirement, I feel like I'm just getting started, at least in some ways. Life is finally opening up for me. I have no idea where my journey will take me or where my capabilities end. I'm still in the discovery process, still learning. Given my age, while I have more potential to tap, I also sense the limitations of time—given my family history, I may have an expiration date that is closer than I would like. Nonetheless, I am overflowing with gratitude for who I am, who I've been, and who I will be. My inner toolbox seems packed with possibilities. Every day is an opportunity to reach inside and discover my next goody.

Insights

The Public Speaking Dream Comes True

When I was growing up, my mom often said, "Someday, you'll even give speeches!" I always laughed it off; it seemed so ridiculous. At the time, I couldn't even read or talk by myself without stuttering up a storm. But I have to admit that when a big family event would come up, I would secretly imagine that I gave a moving speech at the gathering. Still, I never thought that dream would come true.

Comedians like to point out that public speaking is more feared than death. For years, I was one of the fearful, especially after a ten-minute talk took twenty-eight minutes to deliver in my mid-twenties. Even just speaking in a group of friends was often too much for me; it felt like I had a thousand spotlights beating down on me. Nonetheless, decades later, when I was faced with my first five-minute talk for the nonprofit in my position as president, I was terribly nervous and shaky at first but ended up loving the experience, and I couldn't wait to do another. That was my start.

Now I do public speaking and sometimes even get paid for it. Yes, public speaking is a dream come true for me. Not just because my mom used to talk about it or I used to dream about it; no, it's more than that. It's because every speech is a celebration of turning trauma into triumph. It's a testament to everything I've learned about stuttering. It's all there. Think of it: I public speak with BEP; I do the opposite of being rigid by playing with my speech and giving to the audience; I do the opposite of time pressure by taking long, dramatic pauses; and I do the opposite of anticipating stuttering by saying exactly what I want to say.

Given all of that, it's not surprising that often after I give a speech, I walk out of the room, take a deep breath, and express my profound thanks for the ability to freely express myself, convey my message, and connect with an audience. The sense of gratitude never gets old.

Stuttering Proved to Be a Gift

For the first decades of my life, I thought I was cursed. Why was life so hard for me and so easy for others? I suffered helplessly in the clutches of stuttering, so caught up in survival mode that I couldn't see my way out. I couldn't see that maybe there was another side to my challenge. That's how stuttering can be, obscuring your vision, sometimes even smothering all hope. But it doesn't have to be that way. You can address your stuttering and find your way forward.

Now that I have emerged through to the other side, I can see that stuttering was truly a gift. It gave me a challenge to address, a goal to strive for, and a drive to be more than I was. Yes, by itself and left unaddressed, stuttering was indeed a curse. But once I addressed my stuttering and made some real progress, I could see the gift take shape. Pushed to dig deep into my inner toolbox to solve difficult speaking situations, I unearthed capabilities hidden inside myself, became much more resourceful, and discovered the rewards of giving to others. In retrospect, stuttering made me better: it *was* a gift.

Insights

Without stuttering, I may have been a very different person. Perhaps I would have been more successful materially, but I wonder how much I would have liked that person. I think I would have been arrogant and self-absorbed. As I'm reading the last sentence, I am amazed to realize that while I was stuttering, I was arrogant and self-absorbed. That was me. That was my act to keep from feeling all the pain I endured.

That changed in the improvement process. When I finally faced my challenge and began to make progress, I started to discover new things about myself. Life became an adventure. Imagine how exciting it was to relearn to speak, retrain my brain, build confidence, and climb my hierarchy. As I reached the upper rungs of my hierarchy and took on speaking situations that once paralyzed me, it felt like I was knocking down doors. It was exhilarating; I had never felt such a high. Picture my surprise at discovering my inner toolbox, reaching inside myself to find strengths and a resourcefulness I never knew. I gained insights that startled me and felt the joy of transformation from wallowing in the muck to feeling free and marveling in green vistas of opportunity.

These are the raw joys of life. I don't think I would have experienced any of them without being faced with the challenge of stuttering. I wouldn't have had this extraordinary opportunity for growth and the profound sense of gratitude that came with each point of progress. Nor would I have had the opportunity to turn my experience into a way of helping others. It's still strange to me that I discovered what I really love doing—giving—so late in life and that I spent most of my years doing the exact opposite. It's all been a very big surprise to me. Without stuttering, I probably would never have experienced any of this.

To think that I nearly gave up on my stuttering and settled for a life of compromise. To think I could have missed all this: the journey, the learning, the joy. And now, the thrill of helping others with their stuttering—I never could have imagined that possibility. I also never could have imagined that my greatest challenge would become my greatest triumph, maybe even my greatest strength. I am profoundly grateful for it all.

Stuttering can be a gift as long as you face it and work through it. Suffering from the lows, grinding through challenges, and making it to the other side are the essence of human triumph. There may be no better feeling. Now, it's your turn to take on stuttering; it's waiting for you. Take the challenge, appreciate the grind, treasure the gift. Make it yours.

Seek a Partner

Working through challenges can be a lonely battle. You may find it helpful to seek a partner or a support group, either in person or online. In my case, I found a different sort of partner. Let me explain.

Stuttering was so frustrating for me. I had a victim mindset; I felt cursed. Desperate thoughts echoed through my mind: *Why me? Why did this have to happen to me?* The angst eased somewhat when I got married, had kids, and became more engaged in the work world. But still, stuttering hung over me like a mass of foreboding clouds. There didn't seem to be any end to it.

When I started the big push to improve my speech in my mid-fifties, I still harbored some elements of my victim mindset. Sure, I was making progress, but my victim mindset seemed to limit my advance. It was holding me back. How could I possibly become a confident speaker while acting like a victim? The two couldn't coexist; something had to change.

That's when I turned once again to the opposite strategy. I wondered, *What would be the opposite of the "why me" victim mindset?* The answer: to be grateful. Rather than feel cursed by stuttering, I was determined to be thankful for everything I had. This wasn't a passive event; I actively sought things for which to be thankful. It was an eye-opening experience. I realized that I had a lot to be grateful for.

Just as small steps can snowball into big changes, expressions of gratitude—even for seemingly insignificant events—can become deeply meaningful. There may be insignificant events in our lives, but there are no insignificant expressions of gratitude. Eventually, this exploration into gratitude set the stage for a deeper, more meaningful form of expression.

I always felt a connection to God, perhaps born from my desperate circumstances. Now, that connection has been raised to a much higher level. For decades, I felt that I was battling stuttering by myself—me against the world—a losing battle at that. It was a lonely fight; I was outmanned and outgunned on every front. That changed when I began to invest myself seriously in improving my speech and felt a bit of progress. I started to sense that I was no longer alone in this fight.

I began to feel as if I had a partner. A gentle force guiding me through murky waters, feeding me solutions when I started to stumble. Climbing my hierarchy, I could feel God spurring me on to new heights. It was as if I were on a mission from God, and this was my calling: to work through my speech. Call it an inner toolkit, call it what you will; for me, it was as if God were handing me one tool after another to work through my stuttering and keep me moving forward on my path, His path.

Frankly, I was often surprised and amazed at the solutions I developed. Believe me, I was never that resourceful, never that clever. Suddenly, I seemed to be infused with a new host of capabilities so strikingly different from my past that I couldn't help but feel that I was no longer alone in this endeavor. I had a partner. Alone, I was fragile. In partnership, I became much more than I ever was. Our partnership gave me purpose, resilience, and persistence. I wasn't just trying to improve my speech for myself; it was bigger than that, more significant. It was a mission, our mission together. I gave; God gave more. God is the ultimate partner.

The Partnership Evolves

The partnership continues to evolve—it's not just about improving myself anymore. Now I have a new mission: to help others who stutter. I never could have imagined this mission years ago; now I can't imagine my life without it. I have been given the gift of becoming free to speak, and now I feel a pressing obligation to share that gift.

Helping others is new for me; I was always the one desperately seeking help. But this process has changed me and thrust my life in an entirely different direction. What started as a single video one early Sunday morning, minutes after waking up, still dressed in the T-shirt I slept in, has grown into a blog/website, sites on Facebook, Instagram, YouTube, and TikTok, as well as public speaking opportunities. Writing this book is part of that mission.

So is mentoring, which has become my greatest joy (aside from my family). When I climbed to the top of my hierarchy and finally felt free to speak, I thought that was the biggest surprise of my life. And it was. But now there's a very close second: the joy of helping others improve their speech. I relish partnering with people as they work through their challenges, achieve their goals, and live their dreams. It's an honor to be a part of their growth, and I treasure every step of their success.

There have been so many mentoring successes, much more than I expected. Here are a few: the tech analyst who was about to quit his job because his stuttering held him back so badly, now has advanced in his company and even gives internal presentations on new technologies; the woman who always dreamed of a job that would let her see the world but couldn't get through an interview, now works on a cruise ship in Europe; and the executive who used to have sleepless nights in advance of group meetings with the top brass, now handles high-pressure presentations with confidence. Each with a different situation, each found a way forward. There is always a way forward.

As much as I may help them, they have helped me more. The people I mentor bring out the best in me. Their questions and challenges create profoundly personal moments, pushing me to develop concepts and mine thoughts well beyond any I have ever had—perhaps it's the partnership once again rising to the fore. The people I mentor have become my oxygen, my juice, my friends; I cannot thank them enough.

Frankly, I don't know where this mission is headed. It's still evolving. The process seems to be leading me forward, just as I experienced with the effort to improve my speech. Sometimes I'm driving the bus; sometimes I'm just a passenger. Either way, the partnership marches forward.

I often question whether anyone will read this book. Some have tried to console me with the thought that even if it helps just one person, then it would be worthwhile. I find that hard to accept. One person is not the mission. It has to be more than that. It has to help a significant number of people who stutter and the therapists who serve them. It has to spur change.

People who stutter need to know that improvement is possible and that they can fully express themselves without compromise—they can live their dreams. And more speech therapists need to embrace those aspirations, too. Right now, stuttering is holding back too many people. It doesn't have to be that way. Change is possible. People who stutter can become free to speak. That's the mission; that's our partnership. I know the mission won't end with me; I only hope I can give it a good push forward.

Insights

One More Thing

Whether you stutter, you're the parent of a person who stutters, or you're a speech therapist, I hope you have found this book helpful. I have given you everything I've learned in my fifty years of stuttering, my nearly two-year journey to improve my speech, and my years of mentoring people who stutter. It's the best I can do.

Now it's your turn. If you stutter, I hope this book gives you a roadmap to help you improve your speech. If you're a parent, I hope this book gives you insights into helping your child. And if you're a speech therapist, I hope this book gives you ideas that will help your clients. Moreover, if you're thinking of becoming a speech therapist, I hope this book inspires you to enter the field—we need you.

In any case, I just want to help. If I can help you in your stuttering journey, please contact me. I am here for you.

Appendix 1: Roadmap for Improving Your Speech

HERE'S A VERY BRIEF ROADMAP to improve your speech based on my experiences, with some explanation below:

1. Face Your Challenge

2. Establish Your Mechanics and Make Them Automatic

3. Address the Psychological Aspects

4. Construct Your Hierarchy

5. Stack Small Successes and Build Confidence

6. Help Someone Else

Roadmap for Improving Your Speech

1. Face Your Challenge

Realize that stuttering doesn't happen to you—you're the one stuttering, and you're the one who can improve your speech. Own it. Take responsibility for it. Think of it: you've been stuttering for nearly your entire life; it's going to take a herculean effort to move the needle and improve. Make a full commitment to that effort. You may not think you're capable of launching an all-out effort, you may not think you're ready, and that's okay. Once you start making progress, the process will gradually change you. You just need to get started, take the first small step, win it, and take that next small step.

Steps:

- Decide to talk more and engage with the world.

- Take responsibility for your stuttering and own it.

- Make a total commitment to move forward.

- Break the victim mindset.

2. Establish Your Mechanics and Make Them Automatic
Give up your old way of talking and relearn to speak. For me, I thought it made sense to speak like a professional speaker; that's how I landed on BEP. Whatever speaking strategy makes sense to you, practice it so much that it becomes automatic so you don't have to think about it. Relearning to speak won't make you a fluent speaker, but it will give you a solid foundation for making future improvements in your speech.

Steps:

- Learn BEP. Refer to my demonstration video at SteinOnStuttering.com or on YouTube.

- Practice BEP in the privacy of your own room. Read a couple of paragraphs, then summarize for a minute at least three times per ten-minute session, more if you can. Read, then talk, over and over again. Practice early in the morning and late at night, and squeeze in another session during the day. You cannot do too many reps.

- Give up your old way of speaking and make BEP the only way you talk.

- Don't focus on fluency; focus on building your skill in using BEP.

- Be as expressive as you can and generate continuous airflow.

- Practice BEP so much that you make it automatic.

3. Address the Psychological Aspects

Years of stuttering create what I call "stuttering inclinations," the things you do in the stuttering process, such as avoiding speaking situations and switching words to avoid stuttering. You need to break those destructive inclinations, the psychological aspects of your stuttering. For me, the most effective way to do that was to recognize the inclination in real time and do the opposite. If you can do the opposite time after time, you will eventually chip away at that great monolith of stuttering.

Steps:

- Recognize your stuttering inclinations.

- Break your inclinations by doing the opposite.

- Stop the snowball effect of stuttering by stopping midway through a block, going back to the beginning of a phrase, and doing the cleanest BEP you can.

- Play with your speech by having fun talking.

- Take the offensive by pulling the levers of BEP and pushing yourself to be as expressive as you can.

- Break the anticipation cycle by gaining trust in BEP and ending the use of word substitution and filler words.

- Make the goal of every conversation to give and enjoy.

- Take joy in becoming a giver.

4. Construct Your Hierarchy

Construct a hierarchy of your speaking situations. Start with the easiest situation—something so easy you're sure you can win it—and keep adding modestly more challenging situations to your list. Make the steps as small as possible, especially in the beginning. We want wins, not heroes. Don't try to short-cut the process by trying heroic leaps; it's bound to backfire and cause you setbacks. The strategy is to take one small step at a time and stack as many small successes as possible in rapid succession toward your goal so you can build confidence.

Steps:

- Start by listing your two easiest steps at the bottom of the page, your two hardest steps at the top, and fill in as many steps as you can in between.

- Make sure your first steps are so easy that you are confident you can win them. Especially at the beginning, more than anything, you want to stack small successes.

- Stick with small steps and stack small successes in rapid succession.

Roadmap for Improving Your Speech

5. Stack Small Successes and Build Confidence

In the past, confidence has been elusive for you; this process may end that frustration. Make your first step so easy that it's a slam dunk. Win it. Then take your second small step and win that too. Keep taking small steps and stack so many small successes in rapid succession that you build confidence and eventually develop the success habit, the feeling that you expect success every time you speak. Keep climbing your hierarchy one small step at a time toward your goal, and maintain that discipline even if you are tempted to take a leap. This is the way forward to build true confidence, the kind that lasts. Don't stop climbing until you achieve your goal.

Steps:

- Continue taking small steps to stack small successes in rapid succession.

- Add steps to your hierarchy to keep each step small and in a natural progression.

- Develop traction, which is the resilience to keep setbacks manageable.

- Stack so many small successes that you develop the success habit and build true confidence, the kind that lasts.

- Gain the feeling of being unstoppable; the belief that you can take on any speaking challenge that arises.

- Achieve your ultimate goal.

Let's add one more very important point:

6. *Help Someone Else*
Once you've reached your goal, don't stop there. Help someone else. Getting to know other people who stutter and helping them is a great way to reinforce your progress, eliminate your victim mindset, and gain fulfillment. Be a giver. Few joys are greater than helping someone who shares the same challenge you have. Take delight in giving. Give, give, give.

Appendix 2:
Answers to Twenty Questions about Stuttering

THROUGH MY PERSONAL MENTORING, my blog, and my Facebook and Instagram sites, I get asked a lot of questions. Here are some of the most frequently asked questions about stuttering, followed by my answers, many of which you have already seen in this book.

1. How can I overcome stuttering?

If you're a mature-aged adult, you probably can't. Most people think I have overcome stuttering—I have not—I still have my moments now and then, though they are minor and usually insignificant. After stuttering for decades, it's probably unrealistic to think that you could wipe the slate clean and be perfectly fluent. Don't focus on fluency, at least not initially. It's much healthier to focus on improvement and view fluency as a byproduct, the result of your efforts. While you probably won't be able to solve your stuttering entirely, you can improve your speech, achieve your goals, and live the life you want. As I like to say, there may not be a solution, but there is always a way forward.

2. I'm really focused on my speech. Why is my stuttering getting worse?

I often bristle now when I hear that people who stutter should focus on their speech. Why? Because quite often, that means they are focused on fluency, and that is likely to be frustrating, especially in the early stages of improvement. That's why so many people find their speech gets worse in the early going. Instead, focus on developing the skill of BEP and try to have fun speaking. Be as free as you can with your speech. Take the pressure off yourself. Stop focusing on your speech and your fluency; instead, be a giver. Focus on others and what you can do for them. Rather than grade yourself every time you talk on the basis of fluency, focus your evaluation on how much you enjoyed the conversation and what you gave to the other person. Better yet, don't grade yourself at all and just enjoy talking.

3. My problem is that my mind moves faster than my mouth. Is that why I stutter?

I was told this when I was young. It made me feel good about myself, thinking I was so smart. But now, in retrospect, I realize that it's a ridiculous statement. I wasn't smarter than anyone else. My mind moved so fast because I was always anticipating blocks and trying to substitute words to avoid stuttering. You need to break the anticipation cycle and stop substituting words; both subjects are discussed in the next two answers. Once I worked through the anticipation cycle and stopped substituting words, my mind slowed down and a wonderful state of calm emerged within me. As for why you stutter, I have no idea, and neither does anyone else. Forget the why, and focus on improvement and having fun talking.

4. How can I stop anticipating that I will stutter?

Expecting to stutter on certain words and sounds fuels the anticipation cycle. Anticipating stuttering consumed me day and night and led me to substitute words and stick in filler words. Unfortunately, it's a very common problem. Here's how I changed it. I made BEP automatic and gained confidence in my speaking mechanics as I climbed my hierarchy of challenges. Over time, I learned to trust my speaking mechanics so much that I felt I could get through any phrase with BEP. If I could breathe it, I could say it. When you can do that, you will no longer need to be on the lookout for blocks. At that point, you may feel so confident that you can let the anticipation cycle go and free yourself to speak. Sure, you might stutter more at first, but it's a small price to pay for getting rid of the anticipation cycle.

5. Substituting words seems to help me stutter less. Isn't that good?
You may think that substituting words helps you stutter less, and it may now and then, but that short-term gain will be dwarfed by the development of long-term fears. Think of it: When you substitute words, you are effectively telling your brain you can't say that word, which sets up a roadblock every time you think about saying that word or its related sounds. Those innocent attempts to avoid stuttering can turn into fears that last a lifetime. Better to stutter now than create long-term issues. That's another reason why you should master BEP and make it automatic so you can build enough trust in your speech to believe you can stop substituting words and simply say what you originally intended to say.

6. How can I stop stuttering on certain words or sounds?
The popular approach is to practice those words or sounds, but I think that makes the problem worse by making a mountain out of a molehill. Instead, here's what I did: I changed my focus. I stopped focusing on words and sounds, and changed the focus to phrases. I spoke phrase to phrase, breath to breath. In this sense, words and sounds were irrelevant. They were simply widgets that floated on top of a waterfall of air that rose from my stomach and up through my mouth. Every phrase was the same; they all consisted of Breathe, Emphasize, Phrase. When you speak phrase to phrase, breath to breath, you'll find your concerns about certain words and sounds will eventually dissolve because they're irrelevant. You'll only care about phrases—words and sounds no longer matter.

7. I'm so nervous when I talk. How can I become more calm?

Just about everyone gets nervous at some time; it's a part of life. I found it helpful to lower my set point by cutting out caffeine, exercising, and finding other ways to live a generally more relaxing life. But that's just the start; it isn't going to eliminate your anxiety entirely, especially when you're talking in the heat of a moment. So, I have learned to use up my nervousness by taking BEP to the next level, which I call BEP Extreme. I shorten my phrases to make myself breathe more often, take more full breaths, increase my expressiveness, exaggerate the emphasis of words, play with the length of pauses, use hand gestures and smile as I talk. I still use these strategies in anxious moments, such as at the start of a presentation. With these strategies, the more I talk, the calmer I become. I know this must sound hard to believe, but speaking is now one of the most relaxing things I do in my life.

8. How can I build confidence in my speech?

Affirmations or a positive mindset can foster confidence, but you need to do more to gain true confidence. Your brain is a tough taskmaster: You need to prove success to your brain with actual positive experiences. Take small steps, starting with the easiest steps first, and stack one success after another as you climb your hierarchy of challenges. Stacking successes in rapid succession enables you to build confidence and gradually change your expectations from failure to success, creating a success habit. This is the way forward for building true confidence, the kind that lasts.

9. When I talk, I always feel like I'm out of control. How can I control my stuttering?

Controlling your stuttering is a losing proposition because it leads you to hold on too tight and become rigid with your speech. Instead, do the opposite: Free yourself. Surrender. Let go of your stuttering. Break your rigidity. Instead of trying to control your stuttering, take control of the various levers available to you with Breathe, Emphasize, Phrase. In this way, you dictate the action; you're not waiting for stuttering to overcome you. As I've said, take control or be controlled by stuttering. The more you play with the levers of BEP, the more expressive you will be. Forget about control; have fun and play with your speech.

10. I stutter a lot. Should I choose a career that doesn't require much talking?

No, absolutely not. Work hard and rise to the challenge of the career you want. Don't avoid the career of your dreams to avoid stuttering; that's what I did, and it led to terrible frustration. I felt like I was wasting my life. Instead, go after your dreams. Take ownership of your speech and don't hold yourself back from talking or your career plans. I found that the workplace is one of the best environments for improving your speech because it can provide such a wide range of speaking opportunities. Don't shy away from any career. In recent years, I have met successful people who stutter in medicine, law, business, and so many other fields. Be like them, not like me (for most of my life, anyway). Don't let stuttering hold you back. Find your way forward.

Answers to Twenty Questions about Stuttering

11. My stuttering gets much worse when I talk with people of authority. How can I handle that?

This is very common. Speaking with authority figures is probably near the top of most people's stuttering challenges. It may help to check the reality of this fear. The reality is that people are people. Think of it: In ten or twenty years, you may be a person of authority—why should you be nervous now; you'll be one of them someday. When you rise up to a position of authority, would you want other people to be nervous speaking with you? People of authority are just like anyone else. If you feel nervous, do things that will naturally calm you, such as shorten your phrases to breathe more, play with the length of your phrases and the pauses in between, take more full breaths, and be very expressive. I also like to use humor to level the playing field. Don't focus on your speech and make it a test; instead, place the focus on enjoying the conversation and giving what you can.

12. How can I handle the fear of stuttering?

Stuttering causes fear in so many ways, such as the fear of not being able to say what you want, looking strange, sounding strange, and being viewed as incompetent, undesirable, or worse. While it has become popular to try to simply accept your stuttering and be happy, I was never able to do that. To break down the fear, I realized that I had to face the issue head on and gradually work through speaking situations in small steps of increasing difficulty. In addition, I found that I had to talk as much as I could to shift speaking from being an occasional, scary event to becoming a routine part of my day. By talking as much as possible and climbing my hierarchy one small step at a time, I broke down the fear element, gradually improved my speech, and became more comfortable with speaking.

13. Saying my name is so frustrating! How can I get past that?
This was the hardest thing for me to do, and it was at the very top of my hierarchy. Finally, at the age of fifty-seven, I was able to say my name confidently. But it didn't come easily. After about a year and a half of working through my stuttering, it took several more months to say my name confidently. I tried to view my name as just another phrase, and objectively, that makes sense. But it was so emotionally charged after so many years of traumatic failure that I had to create a separate hierarchy just for this goal.

As usual, I started with the easiest situation—introducing myself to kids—then progressed in small steps to the next easiest situations, such as introducing myself when calling stores and hotels. By the time I moved to in-person introductions—my top goal—I had done a zillion introductions in a wide range of easier situations. Even with all that preparation, introducing myself still proved to be a daunting proposition.

Nonetheless, I hung in there. I did a ridiculous number of face-to-face introductions in rapid succession over a three-week period and was finally able to say my name confidently. That ended it. This accomplishment changed my life more than I ever could have imagined. No longer did I need to hide. I became much more comfortable with my speech and with life in general. While it's tempting to tackle this issue first, I don't think I could have done it successfully without first working through my speech mechanics, the psychological aspects of my stuttering, and an extensive hierarchy of speaking situations. That solid foundation gave me the essential skills and confidence to eventually introduce myself successfully.

Answers to Twenty Questions about Stuttering

14. How can I understand the cause of my stuttering?

I have no idea. This is a popular topic of discussion on the internet, but I think it's largely a worthless endeavor. Unless you had a specific trauma, such as a stroke, you'll probably never know the cause of your stuttering. I have some thoughts about the cause of my stuttering, but there's no way for me to know the truth, and it really doesn't matter. Thoughts about the origin of your stuttering are probably of little value; they won't lead to improved speech, which is what really matters. Stop thinking of the past; focus on what you can do now to improve your speech and your future.

15. How can I give presentations with my stuttering?

Now, I'll surprise you: If you're a person who stutters, presentations may be your easiest speaking situation! Public speaking is how I began my stuttering improvement. I realized that I spoke better when public speaking, so I decided to "public speak" all the time. Think of the advantages of doing presentations: You have control over the pace of your speech, you know the time allowed to give the presentation, and you know your content. Moreover, you won't be interrupted; you can say and do anything you want up there. What could be easier?

Of course, there is the issue of the audience. Here's what I did. Years ago, to calm myself before presentations, I would get to the venue early so I could greet people filing into the room. This would warm up my speaking machinery, warm myself to the crowd, and get me into a comfortable flow of speaking. Then during presentations, I would focus on the friendliest people I could find in the audience—one person on the left, middle, and right—and I would speak directly to them. In a sense, I would speak to three people, not three hundred. I would play around onstage, using a lot of expressiveness and varying the length of my phrases and the pauses in between. Sometimes I would see how long I could pause and hold the audience's attention before they became fidgety.

Don't focus on your stuttering; focus on the audience and have fun with them. Finally, if you have to give a twenty-minute speech, create enough content for seventeen minutes. That will give you a few minutes of cushion to play around with your speech and the audience. By doing that, you won't have to watch the clock, which is a pressure you don't need. Never hurry when you're up there; just go at your own pace, give to the audience, and have fun.

16. *What if I'm asked a challenging question that makes me uncomfortable?*
People who stutter tend to freeze up and get defensive, then jump in to answer a question right away. I sure did. You've got to resist those inclinations. As with all inclinations, do the opposite: smile or laugh and welcome the question. And don't answer right away; instead, deliberate long enough to collect your thoughts and take a fresh, full breath before you start talking. When you finally offer an answer, don't blurt out your words as fast as you can. Again, do the opposite and speak even slower than usual. Take delight in going counter to your inclinations. Take the usual steps to remain calm: shorten your phrases to get in more breaths, take longer pauses between phrases to make sure you always get full breaths, and be as expressive as you can to promote greater airflow. These strategies will eventually use up your nervous energy and make you more calm. No matter what the situation, take control and dictate the terms of your speaking. Realize that you're in complete control, and have fun with it!

Answers to Twenty Questions about Stuttering

17. Why is my stuttering so up and down? How can I change that?
Stuttering seems to go up and down, often depending on what is going on in your life. When you're feeling good and more confident, stuttering appears to fade. But when you're tense or not feeling confident, stuttering often increases. Ideally, it shouldn't matter. We all go through periods of anxiety; it's a part of life. Don't let your mood dictate your stuttering. The words are coming out of your mouth; own the situation and take responsibility for your speech. Feeling down or anxious doesn't mean you have to stutter more. Remember my Michael Jordan Rule? In 1997, Michael Jordan scored thirty-eight points and carried his team to a critical playoff game victory even though he was suffering from the flu (some say food poisoning). You have to be like Michael Jordan: take ownership of your speech, especially when you're not at your best.

If you stutter, you stutter—it's not because of your mood; it's just that you stuttered. No big deal. Own it. Be more consistent with your speech by making BEP automatic. I found that once I made BEP automatic, I still had highs and lows in fluency, but the lows weren't so low. My speech became much more consistent.

In general, go counter to your moods by doing the opposite. When you're down, play with your speech even more. Play with the levers of BEP and be even more expressive. Take delight in going counter to negative emotions at every opportunity, and you'll gradually chip away at the idea that mood impacts your stuttering.

18. I've made a lot of improvement, but sometimes I find myself falling back into old habits. What can I do?
Yes, I know the feeling; little remnants of my stuttering still pop up now and then. It's unlikely, perhaps impossible, to totally eradicate decades of stuttering. When I fall back into my old habits, I smile, sometimes even chuckle, go back to the beginning of the phrase, and do my very best BEP with "the integrity of a phrase" and as much expressiveness as I can muster. If I'm still not back on track, I shorten my phrases to breathe more, increase the length of the pauses between phrases, and play around with my speech through even greater expressiveness. Sure, you may fall back into old habits now and then; it's natural and no big deal as long as you catch it and get yourself back on track.

19. How can I reduce my stuttering at the start of a conversation?
Speaking at the start of a conversation is one of the most challenging times for people who stutter, and it certainly was true for me. I make sure that I start with a particularly full breath and speak on the exhale, almost as if I were about to sing. In fact, I exaggerate that first breath so much that it's almost like I'm announcing, "Hey, I'm going to speak now!" In addition to the big first breath, I will start with short phrases to generate a lot of full breaths, with extra expressiveness and, if appropriate, a smile or a laugh. In short, get that airflow going and be expressive.

Answers to Twenty Questions about Stuttering

20. *My friends talk fast. How can I keep up with them and not stutter so much?*

You probably can't. Don't try to keep up with them; it will usually make you more vulnerable to stuttering. Go at your own pace, not theirs. It may be difficult to do the first time or two, but sticking with your own pace while others speak much faster will mark an important milestone in your improvement. When others speak fast, I take particular delight in sticking with my own pace. In fact, sometimes I go even slower just to prove to myself that I have the ability to go counter to my inclinations. It shows my discipline and not giving in to peer pressure—it's a fun way of showing my strength as a speaker and as a person. Try it. Feel the power. You've earned it!

CONTINUE THE CONVERSATION

Larry views this book as the start of a conversation with his readers. He loves hearing his readers' thoughts on stuttering and facing challenges; they inspire him.

Connect with Larry:
Facebook, Instagram, YouTube, TikTok: @SteinOnStuttering
Blog Website: SteinOnStuttering.com

Mentoring with Larry:
One of Larry's greatest joys is to mentor others who stutter. There is no charge for mentoring.
Contact Larry for mentoring: Larry@SteinOnStuttering.com

Hear Larry Speak:
Contact Larry for public speaking or book club appearances: Larry@SteinOnStuttering.com

Acknowledgments

THE JOURNEY TO IMPROVING MY SPEECH may appear to have been a solitary effort, but it certainly wasn't. I am indebted to the following people in my life and so many more.

I cannot imagine what my parents went through with me, both during my childhood and early adult years. They endured the difficulties but never saw the triumph. I wish I could thank them now for the hope they gave me that kept me going. My mom would say, "You can do whatever you put your mind to," and my dad encouraged me to "Get out there and talk." Both became part of my way forward. Somehow, I hope they know that I turned out all right and their heroic efforts were worthwhile.

I am also fortunate to have loving siblings. My brother's ease of communication set an example of what was possible, while my sister inspired the small steps approach that made this all possible. My brother's recent passing heightened my awareness of my own mortality, pushing me to finish this book and make it special. I miss him terribly.

I have been incredibly blessed with my own family, and those blessings keep growing as new loves enter our lives. Susan hung in there with me when few women might have; she saved me. Our kids, Joe and Aaron, filled my life with so much joy and continue to do so. I hope my experiences are an inspiration to them and their kids, my precious grandchildren. I'm sure it's not a coincidence that the first time I felt free to speak was with Susan and then Joe and Aaron; that's how deeply I love my family.

I have also been fortunate to have input on this book from several generous experts. The always-sage Phil Schneider, a well-known SLP, suggested that the book be a narrative rather than a how-to book—great advice. Neil Pliskin, a highly acclaimed neuropsychologist, offered his comments on the psychological aspects of the book. I also incorporated comments from two other well-known SLPs: Uri Schneider and Kristin Chmela. In addition, I appreciate the input of My Word Publishing and its consultants who helped shepherd this project: Polly Letofsky, Amanda Miller, Bobby Haas, Jennifer Jas, and Victoria Wolf.

Also, I would like to thank Clancy Fine for her photo of me; I'm so happy that she was the photographer. Thanks again to everyone for their contributions.

Finally, I am deeply thankful to the people I mentor who stutter. They have become my inspirations, my oxygen, and my friends. I treasure them all; they give me life. So many of the insights in this book arose from our meetings together. Countless times I interrupted our sessions to say, "Wait, I have to put that in the book!" I hope I have had a positive impact on their lives; they have surely had a profound impact on mine.

This book had many influences, and I am thankful for all of them, including those I may not have mentioned.

About the Author

LARRY STEIN STRUGGLED with stuttering for fifty years, compromising his career and suffering debilitating depressions. In an effort to save the business of his dreams, he launched a drive to improve his speech that far exceeded his expectations. Over the next two years, he relearned to speak, retrained his brain, and worked through speaking situations that once paralyzed him. Today, he runs his dream business, is a professional speaker, and mentors people who stutter on nearly every continent of the world at no charge. He currently lives in a northern suburb of Chicago with his wife. They have two adult children, both married, and two grandchildren (so far). Active in the stuttering community worldwide, he writes and posts videos on his blog, SteinOnStuttering.com, as well as his YouTube, Facebook and Instagram channels of the same name. To hire Larry to speak at your event, contact him at Larry@SteinOnStuttering.com.

Don't Forget Your
FREE GIFT!

Free to Speak Workbook:
Your Roadmap to Results!

You've read the book, now put the words into results! This is your roadmap to be Free to Speak.

In this step-by-step workbook, Larry will guide you with the exact strategies he used, plus links to his videos. Keep learning through Larry's blog and private community.

BONUS:
1 FREE HOUR OF PERSONAL COACHING WITH LARRY

Scan the QR code for Larry's FREE DOWNLOAD
Free to Speak Workbook: Your Roadmap to Results!

www.ingramcontent.com/pod-product-compliance
Lightning Source LLC
Chambersburg PA
CBHW031258110426
42743CB00040B/732